The Truth Behind Gun Control
© Ben Baker 2018
© RedneckGenius Productions 2018
An imprint of
Baker Brothers Easy Handling Watermelon System®

833 S. Main St
Ashburn GA
31714
www.BakerBrosPR.com

ISBN-13: 978-1717220110
ISBN-10: 1717220118

INSIDE

The Truth About Gun Control II

THE TRUTH

Someone much wiser than I once said, "The truth will set you free."

To which I reply, "If the truth hurts, yer living wrong."

This book has truth it in. This book will hurt a lot of people because they are not willing to embrace the truth. Writing this book hurt me a couple of times because I found some uncomfortable truths about guns, gun control and the history of guns in the United States.

Some of the truths in here will also hurt the most ardent gun advocates among us.

Get over it.

I have absorbed this truth. It no longer hurts. Whether I like this truth or not is irrelevant. It is the truth and I must accept it or be delusional.

Ben

Slip Sliding Away

Some people just don't get it. They refuse to see what is happening. Rose-colored glasses must be marvelous things. Of course, they can't hold a candle to the Joo Janta 200 Super-Chromatic Peril Sensitive Sunglasses.

> http://hitchhikers.wikia.com/wiki/Joo_Janta_200_Super-Chromatic_Peril_Sensitive_Sunglasses

Anyway, take off your reality-perception-altering shades and get a dose of realism right here.

Gun control is already on a slippery slope with an increasing pitch and someone squirting grease on the track ahead. Don't believe me? Let's take a walk through time and see how far this slippery slope has carried us.

HERE'S YA PROOF

In the 1700s, if you wanted to make a gun, you did it. It did involve a lot of work under a gunsmith to learn the trade. Government regulation was scant. Government orders for guns were common.

Government still stepped in with confiscation efforts.

"As British troops sailed to Boston in 1768, the Boston Gazette reported that the ministry commanded things 'more grievous to the people, than any thing hitherto made known'" the first of which was 'that the inhabitants of this Province are to be disarmed.' By 1774, the British were routinely conducting warrantless searches and seizures of firearms in the Boston area, leading the Gazette to exclaim that 'what most irritated the people next to seizing their arms and ammunition' was the arrest of patriot political leaders. King George

III ordered the seizure of any firearms imported into the colonies.

https://www.washingtonpost.com/archive/opinions/1995/05/31/when-the-redcoats-confiscated-guns/e38d0810-af85-4949-8d93-3da746601e65/

"This Article reviews the British gun control program that precipitated the American Revolution: the 1774 import ban on firearms and gunpowder; the 1774-75 confiscations of firearms and gunpowder; and the use of violence to effectuate the confiscations. It was these events that changed a situation of political tension into a shooting war. Each of these British abuses provides insights into the scope of the modern Second Amendment."

http://www.davekopel.org/2A/LawRev/american-revolution-against-british-gun-control.html

So der yaggo. This nation created a revolution in part because the government was taking away the guns.

THE NEW NATION

The first draft of the Constitution did not refer to guns. It was added, in the Bill of Rights, because some forward-thinking Founding Fathers said "Hey. We better codify this, even though it should go without saying."

"The Bill of Rights is a list of limits on government power. For example, what the Founders saw as the natural right of individuals to speak and worship freely was protected by the First Amendment's prohibitions on Congress from making laws establishing a religion or abridging freedom of speech. For another example, the natural right to be free from unreasonable government intrusion in one's home was safeguarded by the Fourth Amendment's warrant requirements."

http://www.billofrightsinstitute.org/founding-documents/bill-of-rights/

LICENSED TO DO BUSINESS

Guns were sold and manufactured back then without any permitting or processing requirements for the most part. Some gun makers did have permission from the governments at the time; more of a blessing than permission kind of thing. If you can find evidence to the contrary, please let me know and I will update this.

In one respect a government order for guns could be considered a license to make guns. But the true business license is a more modern convention. Now, if you want to produce anything commercially you must have a license.

"In the late 1930s, the Court repudiated Lochner, thereby rejecting its prior understanding of liberty and ushering in a more active regulatory state." Lochner is a term for the economic age where business was not subject to the amount of government regulation now in place.

https://www.yalelawjournal.org/forum/business-
licensing-and-constitutional-liberty

THE FIRST FEDERAL LAW

The first federal law, not the Constitution, but legislation of the modern firearm era, was in 1934. The NFA - National Firearms Act - was created by Congress.

https://www.atf.gov/qa-category/national-firearms-act-nfa

Until this point, full auto firearms and many more weapons were legal for purchase if you had the money. With the 1934 NFA, a $200 tax stamp was imposed. The Bureau of Alcohol, Tobacco and Firearms (BATF) was in charge of the tax stamp which also amounted to a permit and background check since the BATF could deny the application. This act also put licensing requirements on people who made NFA-eligible firearms and accessories. It also created a national gun registry, something not heard of since Colonial times.

https://www.atf.gov/rules-and-regulations/national-firearms-act

MORE LICENSES

In 1938, the Federal Firearms Act required licenses for firearm dealers.

http://time.com/5169210/us-gun-control-laws-history-timeline/

MAIL ORDER GUNS

Lee Harvey Oswald, famed killer of JFK, bought a gun mail-order in the 1960s. After the assassination, the law was changed. Mail order firearms were not allowed anymore. With this came background checks, more licenses and regulation. "Under federal law, any interstate firearms sale -- whether the seller is a licensed dealer or private individual -- must be concluded by a licensed dealer with a background check through the FBI's National Instant Criminal Background Check System."

https://www.ctpost.com/local/article/50-years-after-JFK-mail-order-guns-still-easy-4988480.php

NFA AMENDED

The NFA was amended, changed, modified, added, whatever in 1968. "…1968, the first year the federal government set age limits for gun purchases. Before then, regulation for non-machine guns was mostly left to states. It's not clear whether states had formal age restrictions for guns, but gun access in some states may have followed the 'age of majority,' i.e. the age at which you were considered a legal adult."
https://www.history.com/news/gun-age-limits-history

"First, the requirement for possessors of unregistered firearms to register was removed. Indeed, under the amended law, there is no mechanism for a possessor to register an unregistered NFA firearm already possessed by the person."

https://www.atf.gov/rules-and-regulations/national-firearms-act

This was the second time the feds created a background check. "House Resolution 17735, known as the Gun Control Act, was signed into law by President Lyndon B. Johnson on October 22, 1968, banning mail order sales of rifles and shotguns and prohibiting most felons, drug users and people found mentally incompetent from buying guns."

https://en.wikipedia.org/wiki/Gun_Control_Act_of_1968

1968 is also the start of universal serial numbers on guns. Before this, guns could have serial numbers, but it was not required. I have a Trapdoor Springfield made in 1878 that has a serial number. I have a

single-shot .22 carbine made in the early 1960s without a serial number.
The difference? The Springfield was government order rifle. Government needs tracking numbers. The SS .22 was made for the civilian
market.

Which one is more lethal? Both will drop any animal native to North
America in its tracks with one shot. I killed a 1500 pound animal with a
.22 firing .22 shorts. A .22 short is the most anemic powder-fired round
available.

NFA AMENDED AGAIN

The NFA was again amended in 1986, the Firearm Owners Protection Act (the title is proof government lies). "The Act also amended the
GCA to prohibit the transfer or possession of machine guns. Exceptions
were made for transfers of machine guns to, or possession of machine
guns by, government agencies, and those lawfully possessed before the
effective date of the prohibition, May 19, 1986." This effectively banned
the production of FA firearms except for government use.

http://www.atf.gov/rules-and-regulations/national-firearms-act

Ronald Reagan, the liberal president, lobbied for and signed the 1986
legislation. "The Ku Klux Klan, Ronald Reagan, and, for most of its history, the NRA all worked to control guns. The Founding Fathers? They
required gun ownership—and regulated it. And no group has more
fiercely advocated the right to bear loaded weapons in public than the
Black Panthers—the true pioneers of the modern pro-gun movement."

https://www.theatlantic.com/magazine/archive/2011/09/the-secret-
history-of-guns/308608/

Following the president getting shot, "explosive" bullets were
banned, despite what some in the media say. "The report also contained
a preposterous invention: Chicago's criminals, the report said, covet
something called 'R.I.P.' bullets, which are, in the report's words, 'designed to explode inside the body.'"

https://www.nationalreview.com/corner/exploding-bullets-dont-exist-
contrary-kera-claims/

Some people may confuse exploding bullets with sintering or frangi-
ble bullets. A few companies also make projectiles that break apart on

impact, sending bullet pieces on tangential paths. To my thinking, these kinds of ammo is not very effective, except on small game, because the bullet sheds a lot of power in a real hurry.

BUSH I

Bush I approved a law banning the import of certain kinds of guns in 1989. "The Bush Administration declared a permanent ban today on almost all foreign-made semiautomatic assault rifles. Imports of the weapons have been suspended since spring."

https://www.nytimes.com/1989/07/08/us/import-ban-on-assault-rifles-becomes-permanent.html

NICS

What we now know as the "background check," the NICS, was started in 1998.

"The National Instant Criminal Background Check System (NICS) is a United States system for determining if prospective firearms or explosives buyers' name and birth year match those of a person who is not eligible to buy. It was mandated by the Brady Handgun Violence Prevention Act (Brady Law) of 1993 and launched by the Federal Bureau of Investigation (FBI) in 1998."

https://en.wikipedia.org/wiki/National_Instant_Criminal_Background_Check_System

THE GUN BAN

The 1994 The Public Safety and Recreational Firearms Act banned manufacture and import of some specific firearms and accessories. It did not outlaw ownership. The law did have a sunset provision. Attempts to resurrect this law have so far failed.

https://fivethirtyeight.com/features/guns-like-the-ar-15-were-never-fully-banned/

The 1994 act also moved some guns into the Class III category.

TIAHRT AMENDMENT

It is very questionable if the Tiahrt Amendment is pro or anti-gun. "The Tiahrt Amendment, proposed by Todd Tiahrt (R-Kan.), prohibited the ATF from publicly releasing data showing where criminals purchased their firearms and stipulated that only law enforcement officers or prosecutors could access such information."

The reason I say questionable is because once this information is requested, it eventually becomes part of the public record of a criminal investigation.

PROTECTION OF LAWFUL COMMERCE

No question the Protection of Lawful Commerce act is pro-gun. Gun manufacturers cannot be sued in federal or state civil court by victims of gun violence.

Now liberal heads will go all splodey. "Since he launched his campaign, (Bernie) Sanders has taken flak from Clinton and other gun controllers for supporting the 2005 Protection of Lawful Commerce in Arms Act, which bans lawsuits based on 'the harm solely caused by the criminal or unlawful misuse of firearm products or ammunition products by others when the product functioned as designed and intended.'"

Also, that liberal bastion Obama expanded gun rights. "In fact, Obama signed only two major laws that address how guns are carried in America, and both actually expand the rights of gun owners."

HELLER

The 2008 Heller decision at the Supreme Court was a smackdown on gun bans. The High Court narrowly ruled a Washington DC handgun ban was unconstitutional. ""The handgun ban and the trigger-lock requirement (as applied to self-defense) violate the Second Amendment."

https://www.supremecourt.gov/opinions/07pdf/07-290.pdf

IMPORT BAN

In a case of one step forward and a major retreat, in 2014 Obama also blocked importing some guns from other countries. "Executive Order 13661, titled, 'Blocking Property of Additional Persons Contributing to the Situation in Ukraine,' was signed March 16th in response to Russian actions in the ongoing conflict in Ukraine."

https://www.nraila.org/articles/20140717/obama-administration-bans-import-of-popular-russian-firearms

TRUMP TRAIN

The current Liar in Chief has also put the STOMP! of approval on bans. "On June 20, 2017, the U.S. Treasury Department added Molot to its list of Ukraine-related sanctions 'for operating in the arms or related material sector of the Russian Federation and for acting or purporting to act for on behalf of, directly or indirectly, Kalashnikov Concern,' the Treasury Department said in a statement."

https://warisboring.com/trump-expands-on-what-obama-started-banning-russian-rifle-imports/

BANS SINCE THEN

States and some cities have enacted their own bans.

http://thefederalist.com/2018/04/09/absence-supreme-court-review-massachusetts-judge-upholds-sweeping-gun-ban/

"With minor exceptions, state law prohibits giving an assault weapon to anyone; distributing, transporting, or importing an assault weapon; or keeping, offering, or exposing any such weapon for sale. It also, with minor exceptions, prohibits possession of an assault weapon unless the owner lawfully possessed the weapon before the ban took effect and obtained a certificate of possession from the Department of Emergency

Services and Public Protection (DESPP) for it (in effect, registered the weapon)."

https://www.cga.ct.gov/2013/rpt/2013-R-0241.htm

"New York prohibits the manufacture, transportation, disposal and possession of any large capacity ammunition feeding device, which New York law defines as "a magazine, belt, drum, feed strip, or similar device that: 1) has a capacity of, or that can be readily restored or converted to accept, more than ten rounds of ammunition; 2) contains more than seven rounds of ammunition; or 3) is obtained after January 15, 2013 and has a capacity of, or can be readily restored or converted to accept more than seven rounds of ammunition."

http://lawcenter.giffords.org/large-capacity-ammunition-magazines-in-new-york/

Others are trying this too.

HAPPENING RIGHT NOW

Moves to repeal the 2nd Amendment are also on the increase.

http://porkbrainsandmilkgravy.blogspot.com/2018/02/the-great-gun-grab.html

PICKING UP SPEED

The truth is, gun rights are on a slippery slope. Anyone who says otherwise is ignoring the facts here.

Some will insist otherwise. "Nope. No slippery slope here. Nothing to see here citizen. Move along. Uncle Sam will tell you what you need to know and what you are allowed to have."

http://www.foxnews.com/world/2018/04/08/london-mayor-sadiq-khan-targets-knives-as-murder-rate-spikes-there-is-never-reason-to-carry-knife.html

Gun Grabbing Part I

Aaight, so here we are going to look at some very different attacks on guns.

NEED

No one needs a (insert gun type, make, model, color, ammo, manufacturer, etc) gun.

Absolutely correct. 100 percent right. Can be no argument there.

What does a human being need? 4 things really.

A breathable gas, the air in other words.

Potable water.

Food.

Shelter from the elements.

Gun doesn't come into that equation anywhere. Nor does the Internet, TV, YouTube, smartphones, vehicles and, depending on where you live, clothes. S'right. If you live in tropical regions, you don't need clothes. Stone Age tribe do well without the latest fashions.

What we are left with is wants.

THE KILLING FIELDS

Guns are only meant to kill is the claim.

Etymonline checks the origin of the word gun and finds it is linked to war ... and women. "mid-14c., gunne "an engine of war that throws rocks, arrows or other missiles from a tube by the force of explosive powder or other substance," apparently a shortening of woman's name Gunilda, found in Middle English gonnilde "cannon" and in an Anglo-Latin reference to a specific gun from a 1330 munitions inventory of Windsor Castle ("... una magna balista de cornu quae Domina Gunilda ..."). Also compare gonnilde gnoste "spark or flame used to fire a cannon" (early 14c.). The woman's name is from Old Norse Gunnhildr, a compound of gunnr and hildr, both meaning "war, battle."

https://www.etymonline.com/word/gun

GUNPOWDER

Before the gun was the powder to hurl a projectile. Why was the powder created?

Historians a re pretty split over the when where, why and how.

"In 142 AD, during the Han Dynasty, a man named Wei Boyang was the first to write anything about gunpowder. He wrote about a mixture of three powders that would "fly and dance" violently. We aren't sure that he meant gunpowder, but that's the only explosive that uses three ingredients that we know of. He may have been a Taoist trying to find a potion to let you live forever."

https://quatr.us/china/gunpowder-ancient-china.htm

Historians are pretty certain gunpowder was first used for displays. Think fireworks show on the 4th of July. China then figured out this stuff could be used to throw things, like rocks, at enemies. Powder was packed into bamboo tubes and stones dropped in, exactly like today's muzzleloaders, and ignited. Glad I was not holding the bamboo! These things were more along the line of a cannon than what we call a firearm today, but the underlying principal is the same.

THE WEST GETS INVOLVED

Word spread west. When the first modern "gun" came about is not known. Sources range this from the 1100s to the 1330s. "Historians typically recognize Chinese fire lances, which were invented in the 10th century, as the first guns. These bamboo or metal tubes projected flames and shrapnel at their targets. Cannons appeared in Italy around 1320, where they were modified as European nations waged many wars." https://science.howstuffworks.com/innovation/inventions/who-invented-the-first-gun.htm

"The origin of gunpowder is unknown, and may have occurred in China, Turkey, or Europe. The first record describing the combination of charcoal, sulphur, and saltpeter, to produce a rapidly burning or exploding powder is a coded writing by Franciscan monk Roger Bacon shortly before 1250 A.D.

Within 50 years, early cannon had been developed. A large thick metal tube with one closed end (the breech) and an open end (the muzzle) was loaded first with gunpowder and then with a projectile. The powder was ignited with a torch or smoldering ember through a small hole in the rear (the touchhole). The rapidly expanding gases from the exploding gunpowder would throw the projectile from the barrel. This basic principle still applies today."

http://www.nramuseum.com/gun-info-research/a-brief-history-of-firearms.aspx

PUNCHING TARGETS

Pretty clear the object of these things was war. However, war and killing other humans was not the only thing on the minds of people with guns.

"The first shooting clubs were formed by German-speaking peoples in the 13th and 14th centuries. Membership was limited to men only. At first, bows and wheel-lock muskets were shot from the standing position, but by the 16th century, firearms with rifled barrels were used in public matches. Early club competitions were festive one-shot matches fired at elaborately painted wooden targets. Matches and shooting festivals for one or more clubs were routinely held on New Year's Day, religious holidays, and other special occasions. Prizes of gold and money were frequently awarded."

http://www.washingtonpost.com/wp-srv/sports/olympics/longterm/shooting/shthist.htm

You can argue these guns were designed for killing and merely used in target practice.

Today, many guns are made and sold specifically for the express purpose of poking holes in paper at various distances. For instance https://www.anschutznorthamerica.com/match-rifles.html For a discussion on the lethality of the .22 see elsewhere in this fine book.

THE AR15

Some people say the AR15 is only meant to kill people.

The AR15 is the civilian version of the select-fire (full auto) M16, which the military carries. See elsewhere in this book for a discussion on military firearms and whether civilians should have them.

Is the AR15 (and variants) designed to kill people? If you look at the Geneva conventions and other international treaties on how war is conducted, there is no answer. If you look at military reports, the answer is nuanced.

The M16, from which the AR15 was created, was invented by Eugene Stoner. In researching this, I found a lot of stories pointing to an NBC report that claims to interview Eugene's surviving family. I say claim because I do not believe the news report. The NBC story says the family spoke on condition of anonymity. As a professional journalist for 32+ years with more than 100 awards for my work in communications AND my work used in an Australian university, etc etc etc, I tell you this - When a media outlet uses "anonymous sources." it is making stuff up to fit a narrative and a preconceived view.

Yes, I am saying NBC is lying in the report about Eugene Stoner and the rifle he created.

A BRIEF HISTORY

Here's a brief history of this firearm. A 1962 field test report on the Armalite 15 rifle by the military described it as a suitable weapon for the Vietnam native soldiers.

http://www.dtic.mil/dtic/tr/fulltext/u2/343778.pdf

The report said the gun made a good choice for the small-framed ARVN troops because it was light, easy to shoot and clean, accurate and effective.

"The lethality of the AR-15 (the M16 now) and its reliability record were particularly impressive. All confirmed casualties inflicted by the AR-15 (the M16 now), including extremity shots, were fatal," the report says.

At the same time, the same report says the rifle was reliable under all conditions except very cold weather. This is at odds with reports from troops in 'Nam. "What wasn't a rumor were the gun's initial issues with reliability. Over the years legions of barbershop, coffee shop, and internet commandoes have opined on the reasons for the failures and kept alive the memory of those failures. Today there are still people who will tell you that they'll never own a 'Mattel gun' because they're 'unreliable'."

http://www.grantcunningham.com/2015/01/what-happened-to-the-m16-in-vietnam-how-about-asking-the-guy-who-designed-it/

If you read the article, you'll see that the unreliable parts had to do with the powder and other problems. With all that mind, the military report has to be somewhat suspect.

"During those years ('Nam), in which more than 40,000 American soldiers were killed by hostile fire and more than 250,000 wounded, American troops in Vietnam were equipped with a rifle that their superiors knew would fail when put to the test," says a report in The Atlantic from 1981.

https://www.theatlantic.com/magazine/archive/1981/06/m-16-a-bureaucratic-horror-story/545153/

A Congressional hearing was held. A report was issued. "The hearing record, nearly 600 pages long, is a forgotten document, which received modest press attention at the time and calls up only dim recollections now. Yet it is a pure portrayal of the banality of evil."

SPLITTING THE ATOM

Above, I state the idea that the AR-15 is designed to kill people is a nuanced decision. Someone else will say I'm trying to find a divided line so small, I might as well be splitting the atom.

When court decisions hang on a single word, yeah, I'm splitting. When a court uses a single comma to make a ruling

https://qz.com/932004/the-oxford-comma-a-maine-court-settled-the-grammar-debate-over-serial-commas-with-a-ruling-on-overtime-pay-for-dairy-truck-drivers/

yeah, I'm going there. Comma placement, according to some people, is integral to the Second Amendment.

https://www.theatlantic.com/notes/2016/01/most-consequential-comma/426894/

So yeah. Let's split some stuff and get really pedantic. The courts require it. I require it. When are talking about what is a Constitutional Right, yeah we need to get as precise as possible.

NEVER KILLED

The AR-15 and all its variants have never killed anyone, as best I can find. You say I am wrong. OK, show me a case where an AR-15 alone was the cause of death. You can't.

What you can find is, in the military reports, a soldier broke the stock of his rifle beating an enemy soldier with it. We do not know if the enemy died or not. In fact, beating someone to death is more common than you may think.

http://dailycaller.com/2015/09/30/fbi-data-shows-youre-more-likely-to-get-beaten-to-death-than-killed-with-a-rifle/

Also, the Armalite Rifle 15 (the M16 now) was designed for the military. So, yes, this rifle was designed for the express purpose of shooting ammo to kill people. That is what the military does with guns.

THE AMMO

The reality is, the AR-15 is harmless. The real killer is the ammo it uses. The Hague Conventions banned hollow point ammo. Why? Because it creates wounds far in excess of a full metal jacket bullet. A FMJ bullet means the lead is covered with a harder metal, typical copper, to keep it from expanding. In contrast a HP is meant to expand with immense force, sometime fragmenting with near explosive power.

Bullet types -

http://concealednation.org/2015/07/the-differences-between-jhp-swc-
fmj-p-and-others-what-do-these-ammo-types-mean/

FMJ v. HP as carry ammo -

http://concealednation.org/2014/12/i-met-someone-today-who-uses-
target-ammo-fmj-as-carry-ammo-so-yea-theyre-out-there/

FMJ v HP video - https://www.youtube.com/watch?v=7kbFoXJfhIE

Eugene Stoner, according to all the real evidence we have, designed the AR platform to fire a .223 ammo (actual bullet diameter .224 - don't get me started on bullet names compared to actual bullet sizes) FMJ. Why? Because the bullet tumbles, increase damage as it tears through flesh. Larger FMJs just make a straight hole through. See above video.

You can buy .223 ammo in soft point, FMJ and hollow point. The HPs are preferred by varmint and small game hunters. Why? The HP is far more immediately terminal than the FMJ. Much more damage, despite the .223's tumbling.

You'd think as lethal as the .223 round is supposed to be, it should be a preferred hunting round.

It is for small game. It is decidedly not suitable for medium game through dangerous game (DG). DG are critters that can and do kill people; think elephant, hippo, cape buffalo, Kodiak bear, etc. Some hog hunting plantations will not allow hunters to use the .223 platform, despite the popularity among hog hunters, because the .223 does not have the killing power needed on bigger hogs.

Yes, yes, yes, I hear you hunters screaming "SHOT PLACEMENT!" If you are in that group, then hunt with a .22 short. Otherwise, hush and let me make my point here.

Why is the .223 Remington, the ammo most closely associated with the AR platform, not suited for hunting anything much bigger than 50 pound animal?

Because it is in a word, anemic. It does not deliver the punch needed to generate a humane kill. See above and below for a discussion on killing power. Yes, the .223 Rem will kill. But compared to other ammo available today, it is not very good in terms of stopping or knockdown power. - Note for the gun folks; knockdown and stopping power are the exact same thing to me. YMMV -

Lemme put this in more familiar terms.

A finishing hammer weighs a few ounces. Finishing hammers are commonly used in upholstery work.

A sledge hammer weighs 8 pounds.

Both will drive a nail. Given enough time, both will drive a railroad spike.

Say both are moving at similar speeds. Which would you rather be hit with?

The .223 Rem is a finishing hammer at 3-6 ounces. A good deer (medium game) hunting round (ammo) is a carpenter's hammer, which weighs in at 1-2 pounds. A big game hunting round is a mallet 3-4 pounds. A DG round is the sledgehammer.

So the lethality of some of the ammo fired by the .223 autoloaders is a given. Some. Of. The. Ammo. Some will not. Will a golf ball kill you? Possibly.

https://www.youtube.com/watch?v=AaaojCps8KY

BANNING THE AMMO

Under the rules of war - yeah, we are so civilized as humans that we actually have rules of war written down, codified and adopted - firearms are actually regulated. Well, ammo is regulated. Guns are much less regulated.

If you can call what the rules of war say about "regulation." It's much more a case of someone having a vague idea and writing that down in a way to be as confusing as possible.

"The Declaration of Saint Petersburg is the first formal agreement prohibiting the use of certain weapons in war. It had its origin in the invention, in 1863, by Russian military authorities of a bullet which exploded on contact with hard substance and whose primary object was to blow up ammunition wagons. In 1867 the projectile was so modified as to explode on contact with a soft substance. As such the bullet would have been an inhuman instrument of war, the Russian Government, unwilling to use the bullet itself or to allow another country to take advantage of it, suggested that the use of the bullet be prohibited by international agreement. The Declaration to that effect adopted in 1868, which has the force of law, confirms the customary rule according to which the use of arms, projectiles and material of a nature to cause unnecessary suffering is prohibited. This rule was later on laid down in Article 23 (e) of the Hague Regulations on land warfare of 1899 an 1907."

https://ihl-databases.icrc.org/ihl/INTRO/130?OpenDocument

In other words, soft-point and hollow-point ammo are banned on the battlefield. The military uses full-metal jacket ammo. This is ammo in which the lead bullet is covered by a harder metal, like copper. This prohibition continued to be refined over the years. The proscriptions continued to be vague.

"All weapons cause suffering. The critical factor in the prohibition against unnecessary suffering is whether the suffering is needless or disproportionate to the military advantages secured by the weapon, not the degree of suffering itself. International agreements may give specific content to the principle in the form of specific agreements to refrain from the use of particular weapons or methods of warfare. Thus, international law has condemned dum dum or exploding bullets because of types of injuries and inevitability of death."

https://ihl-databases.icrc.org/customary-ihl/eng/docs/v2_rul_rule70

"Unnecessary suffering" appears a lot in these discussions. What does it really mean? Damfino. I'll bet you can find a concrete definition in the same dictionary where you'll find "well-regulated" also defined.

" (A historic inconsistency of the law of war is that while it is legally permissible to kill an enemy soldier, should you only wound him, the wound should not cause unnecessary suffering.) In theory, if an enemy soldier can be disabled by a single bullet from, for example, an M16, then two bullets from an M16 or a round from anything larger may cause unnecessary suffering. The theory pales when considering the lethality of the 20th century battlefield. Statesmen, diplomats, and lawyers, recognizing the impracticality of such theory, wisely have avoided any attempt to define the concept of unnecessary suffering."

https://www.mca-marines.org/gazette/killing-myth

"During the conflicts in the former Yugoslavia, the prohibition of means and methods of warfare which are of a nature to cause superfluous injury or unnecessary suffering was included in the agreements relating to what were then regarded as non-international armed conflicts. In addition, in 1991, Yugoslavia denounced Slovenia's alleged use of "soft-nosed bullets" because they caused "disproportionate and needless injury"

https://ihl-databases.icrc.org/customary-ihl/eng/docs/v1_rul_rule70

Explosive bullets were also banned. "The use of 'any projectile of a weight below 400 grammes, which is either explosive or charged with fulminating or inflammable substances' was prohibited under the 1868 Saint Petersburg Declaration, applicable 'in time of war between civilized nations' (equivalent to international armed conflict). Although the Saint Petersburg Declaration is still formally binding on some states, its practical relevance today lies in the rules of customary international law it sets forth."

http://www.weaponslaw.org/weapons/exploding-bullets

This literally an issue of ammo, not the gun firing the round.

https://www.military.com/daily-news/2015/03/20/army-and-marine-corps-still-disagree-over-m16-m4-bullet.html

http://www.thefirearmblog.com/blog/2016/01/01/spec-ops-doctor-rather-shot-with-ak-47-over-m16/

A question here is: Do the Geneva conventions require combatants to shoot ammo or use guns that will wound rather than kill? Killing enemy combatants is legal under all these accords. It runs right back to that pesky phrase "unnecessary suffering."

Damn politicians being more vague than someone's ex posting a rant on Facebook.

The real question is, are guns designed to kill? Reading the international accords on the rules of war, and more specifically the rules of war as held by the United States, the answer has to be no. Whether lethal force is delivered or not rests on the type of ammo used. This may be riding a technicality, but this is the legal matter I'm talking about.

In that regard, no, the AR15 is not designed to kill.

Damned technicalities!

THE REAL QUESTION

To answer the real question of "are guns meant to kill?," look at this from some different perspectives.

1) Over most of the history of the firearm, yes, most guns were meant to be a device to deal death to other human beings. Few people had a gun. Those who did were expected to serve in the military forces of the time. Yep. Guns are meant to be a tool to kill other people.

2) A gun is merely a tool. It requires a human agent to take action to be lethal. Handguns, explicitly legal according to the Supreme Court, lead the pack when it comes to murders. No. 2? Knives.

https://www.statista.com/statistics/195325/murder-victims-in-the-us-by-weapon-used/

We do not, at least in the US, hear a call for banning knives. Australia has banned knives over a certain size and London's mayor called for a knife ban.

https://www.usatoday.com/story/news/world/2018/04/09/london-mayor-knife-control/500328002/

Few of us demand restricting other tools that lead to death.

3) "21% of teen drivers involved in fatal accidents were distracted by their cell phones. Teen drivers are 4x more likely than adults to get into car crashes or near-crashes when talking or texting on a cell phone."

https://www.edgarsnyder.com/car-accident/cause-of-accident/cell-phone/cell-phone-statistics.html

"Accidents account for nearly one-half of all teenage deaths. As a category of accidents, motor vehicle fatality is the leading cause of death to teenagers, representing over one-third of all deaths," says the CDC.

https://www.cdc.gov/nchs/products/databriefs/db37.htm

4) In terms of modern firearms, no, most guns, at least in the US, are not meant to be a device used to deal death to other human beings. Most guns in the US are meant for hunting, sport shooting and collecting. Some are for self defense. A minority are meant for killing other people and the vast, vast majority of these guns are in the hands of people paid with our tax dollars.

POINT THREE

Guns kill people.

"I keep hearing this fucking thing that guns don't kill people, but people kill people. If that's the case, why do we give people guns when they go to war? Why not just send the people?" Ozzy Osborne

This is certainly a gun control position by the Godfather of Metal, but it also makes the very important point - someone has to be there to pull the trigger.

For a firearm to deal death, a human action must take place.

1) The gun must be manufactured.

2) Ammo must be created.

3) The gun must be loaded.

I am not aware of any earthly being that can complete these three steps, except for a human being. Yes, once made and loaded, lots of critters can fire a gun.

https://www.livescience.com/15120-planet-apes-chimps-shoot-guns.html

https://www.washingtonpost.com/news/wonk/wp/2015/10/27/a-dog-shoots-a-person-almost-every-year-in-america/

OPINIONS ALLOWED

A group of people who are, in some respects, legends in the outdoors penned a piece for the Huffington Post.

https://www.huffingtonpost.com/entry/opinion-ashe-guns-hunting_us_5af04b20e4b041fd2d28bd88

These ... individuals are entitled to their opinion. As am I. In my opinion, this group of individuals are traitors. Traitors to the very platform on which they built careers and reputations. If you bother to read the HuffPo piece, you'll see that several of them are pretty much hall of fame members in the Outdoor Writers Association of America.

"Here's where we would begin:"

Yes. I pulled a single line from their commentary. This piece was crafted, edited, revised and rewritten to a fare-thee-well. A single line bears enormous weight. This infuriates me more than anything else I've included in this book.

They BEGIN here. Begin. This is, therefore, a starting point for them. They do not say how far they would take this. I hope I never find out.

These people are a major reason I will now never join OWAA, despite receiving several invitations to do so. Certainly they are allowed their opinion. I absolutely defend that. But I cannot, will not and shall not abide a professional association with people like this, people who blindly and willingly sacrifice my rights on their altar of ignorance.

ONE MORE THING

One last link in this chapter because I think it is cool -

https://listverse.com/2013/05/02/10-strange-civil-war-weapons/

The problem is guns

Yes, once again you read that right. The problem is guns. Throw bombs in there too because that's pretty much the same thing.

Guns delivered death to hundreds of millions of people.

In just the past century alone, guns were the cause of death for, eh, call it 160 million people.

https://en.wikipedia.org/wiki/List_of_wars_by_death_toll

In the worst single instance of gun-related (we include bombs remember), more than 100,000 people died immediately. Several times that died later as a result of their injuries.
https://en.wikipedia.org/wiki/Atomic_bombings_of_Hiroshima_and_Nagasaki

The problem is guns. We must take immediate steps to restrict ownership of guns

Government must not be allowed to possess guns.

Government-sponsored, government-led, government-ordered shootings account for more than 95 percent of all gun-related deaths.

Leading the list for the past 100 years is the United States, Germany, Russia and China. These governments have ordered the deaths of more people than any other government on the planet.

Government doesn't need guns. If we prevent government from having guns, mass murders will plummet.

In the case of the United States, government of the people, by the people, for the people. Government directed by the people. You and me and the guy who just ducked around the corner so you won't see him looking at you. The US government is who you put into office. They are your employees.

Your employees murder people almost daily.

If you did not vote, you still complicit. If you voted Reboobican or Damnocrat, you are the problem. You are hiring murderers.

How does it feel to be a mass murderer?

Yeah, the problem is guns, guns in the hands of homicidal maniacs like you, people who hire mass murderers. People who demand elected officials who then order deaths by the thousands, hundreds of thousands and millions.

Perhaps you don't need to be allowed to vote. Maybe you should be banned from voting.

Keep guns out of government hands and prevent you from voting and deaths by gun will plummet.

The Problem Is Guns II

Yes. Updated. Again. More information. Here I present the most comprehensive study on guns and gun violence I am aware of,

https://www.ncbi.nlm.nih.gov/pmc/articles/PMC3828709/

shows as gun ownership rises, gun violence rises. Yup. A study of nearly three decades.

"Gun ownership was a significant predictor of firearm homicide rates (incidence rate ratio = 1.009; 95% confidence interval = 1.004, 1.014). This model indicated that for each percentage point increase in gun ownership, the firearm homicide rate increased by 0.9%."

Before the gun grabbers get excited and the gun rights folks draw down on me, read further. Here's where some people start mumbling, morons start celebrating and a handful of folks like me want to say "BEEN TRYING TO TELL YOU THIS!"

"For each 1 percentage point increase in proportion of household gun ownership, firearm homicide rate increased by 0.9%."

"For each 1 percentage point increase in proportion of Black population, firearm homicide rate increased by 5.2%."

AND

"For each 1-SD increase in proportion of household gun ownership, firearm homicide rate increased by 12.9%"

"For each 1-SD increase in proportion of black population, firearm homicide rate increased by 82.8%"

1-SD is one standard deviation. This is more math than I can handle. https://en.wikipedia.org/wiki/Standard_deviation I have asked people to explain Standard Deviation to me, but so far no one has managed to explain it so simply that I can understand.

What I can tell you from reading this report is race, income inequality and violent crimes increase the gun death rate in percentages and numbers far greater than gun ownership. Non violent crime increased the murder rate more than gun ownership. I can also tell you that locking more criminals up dropped the murder rate in a serious hurry.

THE ORIGINAL

So, guns are the problem. But where is gun violence an issue? Fortunately, we have some fairly reliable information about this. We have some pretty good numbers showing clearly what the problem is. More importantly, we have solid facts, empirical evidence, telling us WHERE this problem exists.

Before I 'splain that, I tell you this. Some people have tried to address this situation. They get shouted down. They get shoved aside. They are insulted, denigrated, attacked and most disheartening to me, ignored.

I ain't talking about conspiracy theory fans either. (If you are a conspiracy theory fan, then please go away.)

Jesse Jackson in his famous "cut his nuts out" comment

https://www.independent.co.uk/news/world/americas/black-power-struggle-i-want-to-cut-his-nuts-out-865071.html

was attacking a former POTUS for perceived failures to address problems facing a segment of the national community. He decried the POTUS' response to growing violence in that segment of the community. You do not hear about that much. You just hear the emasculation comment, not the reason for it.

JUST THE AMMO, MA'AM

So, let's lay bare the barest possible facts. Let others interpret, spin, explain, whine and complain as they will. Cry HAVOC! and let loose the dogs of war. Praise the Lord and pass the ammo.

Then turn loose the spirit of UK Prime Minister Benjamin Disraeli and say "There are three kinds of lies: lies, damned lies and statistics."

https://en.wikipedia.org/wiki/Benjamin_Disraeli

NUMBERS ARE RACIST

So what about those statistics?

Numbers, as I am about to present, are racist. Well, racist according to the people who cannot dispute facts and have to turn to invective and rhetoric.

So, as much as I DESPISE this word, I have to use it. I hate the word because dividing people into groups based on melanin content is sheer stupidity of the highest magnitude. We are people. Humans. Homo Sapiens. Period. However, some people will only understand things when broken down into moronic categories. So, on with the moronics.

US population:

https://www.census.gov/quickfacts/fact/table/US/PST045216

Black or African American alone, percent, July 1, 2016, 13.3%

American Indian and Alaska Native alone, percent, July 1, 2016, 1.3%

Asian alone, percent, July 1, 2016, 5.7%

Native Hawaiian and Other Pacific Islander alone, percent, July 1, 2016, 0.2%

Two or More Races, percent, July 1, 2016, 2.6%

Hispanic or Latino, percent, July 1, 2016, 17.8%

White alone, not Hispanic or Latino, percent, July 1, 2016, 61.3%

Got you some numbers? Good.

MURDER IS RACIST

So let's look at another set of numbers and facts and see how murder is racist.

I tried to put these into a table that would come out here. I can't. Numbers make my head parts hurt.

You look at the page

https://ucr.fbi.gov/crime-in-the-u.s/2013/crime-in-the-u.s.-2013/of-fenses-known-to-law-enforcement/expanded-homicide/expanded_homi-cide_data_table_6_murder_race_and_sex_of_vicitm_by_race_and_sex_of_offender_2013.xls

Fair warning. FBI stats are routinely under fire for UNDERREPORT-ING crime, especially where minorities are concerned. Still, it is what we have.

So what you see here is black people kill other people in massively disproportionate numbers compared to the percentage of the general population. Yeah, racist, I know.

The worst offender is black people killing black people. In 2013:

2,245 black people killed 2.491 black people.

2,509 white people killed 3,005 white people.

That is 5,723 people murdered. Black people accounted for 44 percent of the murders. Black people account for 13 percent of the population.

Racist.

Black people account for less than 15 percent of the population, yet commit nearly four times the number of murders as other segments of the population.

I CAN'T HEAR YOU NOW

Where are the talking heads? Where are the interviews? Where the HELL is National Public Radio? Where the HELL is the Damnocratic Party?

Where the HELL are you and why are you not screaming about THESE NUMBERS?

How many inner city mommas have to cry over a casket before you get up in arms (arharhar) about these deaths? A handful of rich kids in an exclusive school in South Florida die and we have a national crisis. Black teens and young men die EVERY FREEKING DAY in our inner cities and you can't be bothered?

Racist much?

WEAPONS

Guns are responsible for 60 percent or the murders.

Looking at the (questionable but what we got) FBI data

https://ucr.fbi.gov/crime-in-the-u.s/2012/crime-in-the-u.s.-2012/offenses-known-to-law-enforcement/expanded-homicide/expanded_homicide_data_table_8_murder_victims_by_weapon_2008-2012.xls

in 2012 of 12,765 murders, 8,855 were done with guns. Narrowing that down, 6,371 were done with handguns. Rifles account for 322 of those deaths. Rifle types are not broken out.

An AR15 is a rifle. Based on the numbers, the AR15 is far less dangerous than a pistol (handgun). So why are you screaming BAN THE AR15?

NEED MORE STUDY

Some people complain the CDC is prevented, by federal legislation, from studying gun violence.

And?

What's to study? People kill people. The CDC needs to concentrate on the pathogens that kill and cripple people. We have all the evidence we need about gun violence.

What we do about it is another matter.

We have plenty of evidence showing where people kill people and who is killing whom. What we are doing about it is another matter.

Take the guns away, people will still people. In those 2012 stats, fully 1/4th of the murders, 3,920, were committed with something other than a firearm.

CALLING 'EM LIKE THEY ARE

The truth is people are screaming for gun control because they are scared. I get that. they are reacting out of emotion, not facts. Gotcha.

More importantly, they are acting out of what so many call "white privilege" because it is white children who are dying.

Scream on. Demand new laws. The fact is, you don't give a damn about the young black people who are dying in our streets. You only care about people who look like you do.

For every child killed in a school shooting, several die in our streets. And you say nothing.

Here is a salve for your conscience -

http://snapjudgment.org/counted-oakland-story .

A Little Knowledge Is A Dangerous Thing

I have tried, and I mean REALLY TRIED, to not write this one. But dammitall, someone must step in with correct information. (sigh)

A few reminders to start this one:

"No one is coming to take your guns."

http://porkbrainsandmilkgravy.blogspot.com/2018/02/the-great-gun-grab.html

"This is about protecting our kids."

http://porkbrainsandmilkgravy.blogspot.com/2018/03/the-problem-is-guns-ii.html

"This is about stopping the killing."

http://porkbrainsandmilkgravy.blogspot.com/2018/02/the-problem-is-guns.html

BAN MILITARY GUNS

Having shot down the top three arguments above, some in the gun grab crowd now say they only want to ban civilian ownership of military firearms.

They do not know what they are talking about. A little knowledge is a dangerous thing. I explain below.

Also, I am using the exact line of reasoning these people use when calling for gun bans. A major difference between me & them is I am using actual facts and reason to back up my points v. empty rhetoric and emotionally laden vitriol. (Well, most of the time anyway.)

In the interest of just hitting the major points, I will skip over a lot of things like swords, rapiers, man-catchers, advances in projectile tech and etc.

NEARLY 1,000 YEARS OF DEATH

Remember Mr. Peabody and Sherman and their time-traveling cartoon show? Mr. Peabody! Fire up The Wayback Machine. We are visiting the 1100s and the most feared weapon ever created by that time, the crossbow.

"Not surprisingly, the highest European authority of the day, the Roman Catholic Church, called for an outright ban on the weapon. And the Vatican wasn't messing around — violating its decree could lead to excommunication, or worse: damnation of the soul. Strong language, to be sure. In fact, for much of the Middle Ages, the crossbow was considered to be one of the most destabilizing weapons in existence, not unlike today's nuclear, chemical and biological weapons."

So, to ban military weapons, we must ban the crossbow.

https://www.telegraph.co.uk/news/2017/03/20/fears-crossbow-terror-attacks-germany-weapon-found-jihadists/

https://www.theguardian.com/uk-news/2018/jan/14/police-hunt-55-year-old-man-in-connection-with-crossbow-attack

FORWARD!

Mr. Peabody! Take us forward good sir!

Smoothbore rifles, which are on the current banned list anyway in the US, except for muzzleloaders... Well, even the muzzleloaders must be banned.

Loading a muzzleloader -

https://www.youtube.com/watch?v=3CEbBv4U71M .

And that is for 1 shot.

"European military doctrine of the time called for the use of smooth-bore muskets as the primary martial firearm. Although less accurate than rifled arms, the smoothbore allowed for faster reloading, since a lead ball slightly smaller than bore diameter could be rammed down the barrel with wadding quite quickly, even as the barrel became fouled from gunpowder residue from previous shots."

For the sake of space, I shall skip over barrel rifling.

According to the "ban military guns" crowd, we must ban muzzle-loading blacktopped rifles. The Brown Bess was issued to the British Army. This is but one example of many.

"It was the standard arm of the British soldier during the American Revolution. Unlike modern weapons, the musket was slow to load, inac-curate and frequently unreliable. The Brown Bess fired round lead balls, some the size of a quarter. With such an inaccurate gun, soldiers were often massed tightly together, firing a shower of lead balls at the enemy. "

CARTRIDGE ROUNDS

Mr. Peabody! We require your services to take us into the time of car-tridge rounds. A cartridge round is self-contained. The bullet, powder and primer are all in one unit. The first cartridge rounds were developed for civilian use. So, banning ammo as being for "military purposes" is not permitted under these rules of engagement.

But we can point to cartridges and guns made for those rounds specifically made for military use.

The shoulder-breaker and moose hammer .45-70 Government is once again popular among shooters. As the name implies, this round was de-veloped by and for the government. But we cannot ban ammo.

We can ban the rifle for which this ammo was developed. The Trap-door Springfield as we call it today was built on government orders for government use. This single-shot rifle is designed to use black powder in the cartridge. Using some modern ammo can cause the rifle to explode. Really.

Single shot is slow to load. The rifle must be opened, the spent brass removed and a new round inserted.

https://www.youtube.com/watch?v=p_A5HUhpZDs

But, this rifle that is more than 100 years old must be banned because it is a military firearm.

I have one. It was probably used to kill Native Americans. Ban it?

Another cartridge we cannot ban is the .30-06. This round was, again, developed by the government for military use. The ammo is on the world's Top 10 list for most popular deer ammo.

The ammo was developed for the Springfield Model 1903 bolt-action rifle. Since this is a military firearm, it can be banned. Never mind the fact that first few years the guns were made in such a way that firing modern ammo in them can cause them to explode. Literally.

It must be banned because it is a military rifle.

Got one of these too, one of the first off the line. I am truly afraid to shoot it because I do not want it exploding in my face.

Lemme point out here legendary Marine Corps sniper Carlos Hathcock used the Winchester Model 70 in .30-06 in Vietnam. This is rifle is also called "a deer rifle" which the military gun ban crowd says they do not want to ban. Functionally, it is no different than the Springfield 1903, except it won't explode with modern ammo.

What is a sniper rifle? Briefly, here. Gonna look at another SERIOUS sniper rifle in a moment.

STILL IN USE

Someone will point out "Hey Baker, these guns are not used by militaries anymore." You certain?

The venerable Mosin-Nagant is *STILL IN USE BY MILITARIES AROUND THE WORLD!*

What is a Mosin-Nagant? A 30-caliber (think .30-06 deer rifle), 5-round fixed box magazine (think .30-06 deer rifle), bolt action (think .30-06 deer rifle) rifle (think .30-06 deer rifle) that started out in Russia made specifically for the military. Other nations started building them too, all for military use.

All for military use. No Mosin Nagant was ever made, except under government contract for government use.

In what will certainly break the extractor (gun humor) of many in the precision shooting crowd who sneer at the Mosin Nagant, it is the most deadly sniper rifle in history based on the number of kills. The world's

top sniper is Lyudmila Pavlichenko, a Russian lady, who used the Mosin. At the time, she was what the world called a feminist.

In form, function, fit, performance and even appearance, the difference between the Mosin Nagant and a modern Savage .30-06 deer rifle is strictly cosmetic. If you are one who says military firearms should be banned for civilian use - and I prove above the Mosin is still used by militaries - pick the one to ban.

I used to have a Mosin made in 1918 and it most certainly was used to shoot Nazis and others. I had one made in China, dropped on the battlefield during the Korean War. It was certainly used to shoot at American and other troops. Did the shooter kill anyone? Dunno. Don't have 'em any more.

By the "military gun" reasoning, they must be banned. Pick which one from the above must be banned.

THE TRUTH

The simple truth is people who call for banning military-style weapons do not know what they are talking about. Most cannot tell a Glock 19 from a silhouette single shot target pistol. They certainly do not know what a military firearm is. When pressed they come up with AR 15, AK 47 and a few other firearms with letters in the name. What about the AR7? Ban it? Why? Ban the M77? Why?

Magazine capacity and the ability to shoot rapidly are also brought up. Mag capacity, as I show above, has little to do with a firearm's lethality.

Firing rapidly?

https://www.youtube.com/watch?v=lLk1v5bSFPw

This was done with a REVOLVER. I've shot full automatic firearms that don't cycle that fast. Full auto means you hold the trigger and it keeps shooting.

HISTORY SPEAKS

"I prefer dangerous freedom over peaceful slavery."

- Thomas Jefferson, letter to James Madison, January 30, 1787

"What country can preserve its liberties if their rulers are not warned from time to time that their people preserve the spirit of resistance. Let them take arms."

- Thomas Jefferson, letter to James Madison, December 20, 1787

"To disarm the people...[i]s the most effectual way to enslave them."

- George Mason, referencing advice given to the British Parliament by Pennsylvania governor Sir William Keith, The Debates in the Several State Conventions on the Adoption of the Federal Constitution, June 14

Don't Know Enough To Shut Up

A little knowledge is a dangerous thing. Having just enough knowledge to know something can lead the person to believe they are a total expert.

You know people like that. They have just a tiny bit of information and suddenly believe they are possessed of all the facts, data and input and can render flawless judgment and opinions.

Think teenagers.

For those lucky enough to mature, this ability to know everything by knowing only a little does wane. As we age, we realize how little we actually know and refrain from spouting off until we get far more information to assimilate.

Some folks never manage to mature and so never learn how little they actually know.

"As for me, all I know is that I know nothing." Socrates.

To explain - we in the journalism biz, especially those of us who work general and generic beats, are expected to know about everything. Literally. Never mind that's unfair, it is what is expected. You can switch the word journalist for generalist and pretty much mean the same thing.

The sad truth is, we don't know everything, but we often act like it.

It infuriates me.

I've also done the same thing, which drives me even further around the bend. GAAAAAAAH!

Journalists take a little information and expand it into a universe-worth of knowledge, getting it wrong in the process.

I have in the past attempted to redress these errors of fact, which has not endured me to many of my brethren-in-words. I'll probably keep doing it, never minding that it tears down my colleagues' tightly held and long cherished belief that they are absolutely correct.

I'm used to being a pariah.

Yeah, I again admit to taking an inch worth knowledge and stretching it to cover a football field, with the results I complain about herein.

Sparking my particular ire today is young journalists (duh!) who are liberal (duh!) and gun control believers (duh!). Invariably when discussing firearms they refer to "high power" guns and most recently a journalist referred to an AK-47 as a "large gun."

It ain't. They ain't.

Cause this is my rant, I'm gonna 'splain even if you don't wanna know. The AK-47 is a light-medium rifle. It's not a tremendously accurate rifle, of middlin' potency and only medium range. What it does have is extreme reliability under harsh conditions, ability to sling a fair, not a lot but a fair, amount of lead in a given direction in short order and simplicity of construction.

It's also 'bout the most common military-style rifle on the planet owing to the fact so many countries have made and continue to make it.

It is decidedly NOT high power NOR is it large. It is a middlin' to fair deer rifle, but not a gun to hunt moose, elk or large bear.

To give you a more concrete example, some time back I spoke to a group of journalists. I produced two rounds of ammunition, a .22 long rifle and a .50 BMG 750 grain FMJ.

I asked them to decide which bullet is implicated in the most murders in the United States. The lowly .22 round holds that record by a long shot. The .50 BMG has never been used in a murder in the United States and has been implicated in one and only one criminal offense and that was one of negligence, not malice.

I ask you what is high power?

Journalists with no experience in handling firearms just attach whatever adjective they feel is most appropriate to their report on a firearm. Reality has nothing to do with it. Such statements calling the AK47 "high power" and a "large gun" only add to the problems legitimate gun owners have.

But the problem is greater than just the discussion on guns. Journalists have the habit of appending modifiers to everything they (we) write. It shouldn't be done in straight news - opinion pieces are different. But we are human. It takes a very strong will and intense effort to keep ourselves out of the stories we write, especially matters on which we are particularly passionate.

The real hell of it is, as journalists we're not really supposed to be experts. We are supposed to find an expert, ask him and report what he says. Our expertise is supposed to be knowing who to ask.

When we, as journalists, start substituting ourselves in the place of real experts the world gets heaping servings of talking heads with cable TV shows who are more interested in slinging insults at the opposition than engaging in an intelligent and rational debate.

When that happens, civil discourse goes the way of the dodo, the woolly mammoth and politicians interested in serving the people rather than serving themselves and the people who fund their campaigns.

The other more insidious problem is people arc given wrong information, factually incorrect, which they accept as the truth. This is worse than not knowing at all.

If there is no knowledge, then it is a blank slate ready to accept whatever is laid down. An easy move.

When the wrong information is in place, it must first be removed which can be a complicated procedure and is often hard to do, sometimes impossible. Then, new information must be put in place.

Brain surgery, physical brain surgery that is, can be much easier to do. You don't have to believe. If you don't believe me, try to reason with a zealot of any stripe. Then come back and tell me which is easier.

The Great Gun Grab Part II

See my blog http://porkbrainsandmilkgravy.blogspot.com/2018/02/the-great-gun-grab.html to get updates on this one.

So, yeah, they are coming for our guns. I hear the screaming "NO! THEY ARE NOT!"

Hey. Don't take my word for it.

It is already happening.

GUN GRAB REALTIES

Get you some gun grab realities, ripped from the news.

Bill intro'd to allow gun confiscation. https://www.congress.gov/bill/115th-congress/house-bill/5717

https://www.washingtonpost.com/national/health-science/five-states-allow-guns-to-be-seized-before-someone-can-commit-violence/2018/02/16/78ee4cc8-128c-11e8-9570-29c9830535e5_story.html

http://krcrtv.com/archive/california-gun-confiscation-law-takes-effect-jan-1-1

https://usatoday30.usatoday.com/news/nation/2008-10-08-nra-katrina_N.htm

https://merryjane.com/news/hawaii-medical-marijuana-gun-ownership-controversy

http://www.kgw.com/mobile/article/news/local/oregon-initiative-would-ban-assault-weapons-require-owners-to-surrender-certain-guns/283-530640255

http://www.thetruthaboutguns.com/2018/03/john-boch/nc-sheriff-candidate-kill-gun-owners-who-wont-give-up-their-guns/amp/

So you say some of these guns are returned.

Some ain't all. Most ain't all.

SHOULDN'T HAVE GUNS ANYWAY

Some people say some of these people shouldn't have guns in the first place. Ah so. What gives anyone the right to determine that?

Shall we jettison the 4th and 5th Amendments along with the 2nd? Is Due Process is just a phrase?

Some point to "medical diagnosis" by mental health professionals which state a person is unfit to have a firearm. I point out that "mental health professionals" have declared homosexuality to be a mental illness. The history of "mental illness" is rife with massive abuses.

Leaning on a ~~science branch of medicine field of study~~ woo factor that relies on a vote to determine what is a mental illness and what is not? If When the standards of "mental health" were are applied to other fields of healthcare, we get jade eggs for the yoni.

"Psychiatry's diagnostic criteria are literally voted into existence and inserted into the American Psychiatric Association's Diagnostic and Statistical Manual for Mental Disorders (DSM). What is voted in is a system of classification of symptoms that is drastically different from, and foreign to, anything in medicine. None of the diagnoses are supported by objective evidence of physical disease, illness or science."
http://www.cchr.org/quick-facts/disorders-voted-into-existence.html

Voting is how we got the people who hold elected office today. How is that working for you?

JACKING THE 2nd AMENDMENT

To some people, taking our guns is more than just a phrase, It is a cause. They are jacking the 2nd Amendment.

https://psmag.com/social-justice/repeal-the-second-amendment-already

https://www.nytimes.com/2017/10/05/opinion/guns-second-amendment-nra.html

https://www.americamagazine.org/repeal-second-amendment

Google "Repeal second amendment" for lots more exactly like this.

OK, so that is the First Amendment speaking there. That's the 4th Estate and people in general doing the talking. Anyone else putting forth the same ideas?

How about a retired Supreme Court Justice pontificating on why substantive changes need to be made?

https://www.washingtonpost.com/opinions/the-five-extra-words-that-can-fix-the-second-amendment/2014/04/11/f8a19578-b8fa-11e3-96ae-f2c36d2b1245_story.html

And AGAIN - https://www.nytimes.com/2018/03/27/opinion/john-paul-stevens-repeal-second-amendment.html

He is gone from the court, yes but you have it in his own words what he believes needs to be done. All it takes is 5 people, five not elected, appointed-for-life people to change things. Congress can pass any law unanimous and the president enthusiastically sign it. The Supreme Court can knock it down with five votes.

Gimme your pet political stand. I can find a Supreme Court decision that you will vehemently disagree with. And yet, that decision is the law of the land, whether you, I or that hacker reading your screen along with you right now agree.

But the Second Amendment is an Amendment!

And?

This nation has repealed sections of the Constitution, including amendments. The 21st Amendment repealed the 18th.

https://en.wikipedia.org/wiki/Twenty-first_Amendment_to_the_United_States_Constitution

Now I tell you a member of Congress introduced legislation to repeal the Second Amendment

https://www.govtrack.us/congress/bills/103/hjres81/text

Also, a lot of people want it repealed.

https://d25d2506sfb94s.cloudfront.net/cumulus_uploads/document/h8n9gvrqyj/econTabReport.pdf

TAKE OUR GUNS

Some have the temerity to say "No one is coming to take your guns."

Proof to the contrary is hereby presented above. These people are also extremely serious about this.

LIVING IN AN OXYMORON

Some deny this reality. Some will certainly deny this reality. You may live your oxymoron in any way you see fit.

Reality is under no obligation to conform itself to your expectations.

If the truth hurts, yer living wrong.

Do not expect me to accept your version.

Here's a reality for you. People are bizarre. We - you, me certainly, your BFF, your stalker - can hold totally contradictory ideas at the same time and see no problem with this. Living an oxymoron is just another day in this hell of a paradise or this paradise of hell.

Some of you may say there is no way government could confiscate all those weapons. It would be impossible, you say. You are the same people who say there is no way we gun owners could stand against the might of the US military.

Which is it gonna be? Government won't take our guns or we can't stop them from doing it? These are mutually exclusive ideas. Either

government can take our guns OR we gun owners can rise up and over-
throw the government.

Pick one. Except you won't. Rose colored glasses? How about Joo
Janta 200 Super-Chromatic Peril Sensitive Sunglasses, a towel wrapped

around your head and the covers pulled over your head?

VECTORING AGAIN

Approach this from another angle. Show me, please, any government
that has voluntarily relinquished power and backed down without physical force being applied. I don't mean over minor matters. I mean giving
up and quitting. Abandoning the effort. Show me any government that
has ever undergone a substantial reduction in size, scope and power
without physical force applied against it.

If you can find one, and a few exist, I'll show you dozens of examples where only physical force caused the substantive changes. Those
few I said do exist? They underwent voluntary reduction after spending
years of bloody conflict. Guns were involved.

Can't happen today? You are not reading international news. But
that's another topic for another day.

Repealing The Second

In a FB thread a longtime friend asked me to explore the idea that the Second Amendment was repealed.

The Second Amendment as passed by the Congress:

A well regulated Militia, being necessary to the security of a free State, the right of the people to keep and bear Arms, shall not be infringed.

As ratified by the States and authenticated by Thomas Jefferson, Secretary of State:

A well regulated militia being necessary to the security of a free state, the right of the people to keep and bear arms shall not be infringed.

That comma is important. Think not?

https://www.cnn.com/2017/03/15/health/oxford-comma-maine-court-case-trnd/index.html

"We already know punctuation saves lives. Now a Supreme Court ruling proves it also makes or breaks legal cases."
http://www.newser.com/story/221425/scotus-upholds-guys-porn-sentence-based-on-a-comma.html

Anyway. could the Second Amendment be repealed? Sure. When you consider the intellectual level of the United States taken as a whole is on par with a retarded flatworm, anything is possible.

However, it's is unlikely to happen any time soon. A repeal requires a vote of a majority of states' legislatures. 25 or so states now have a State Constitution guarantee that hunting and fishing is a right held by the people. 49 states now have laws in place allowing citizens to carry a firearm. Illinois is the holdout. These regs do vary with Alaska being the freest - You got it, tote it - to some states requiring training and limiting the places where a gun can be carried.

Which does not answer the question. If the Second Amendment is re-pealed by popular vote, this means a fundamental shift in American atti-tudes toward firearms. Somewhere around 80-90 percent of the populace agree people who be allowed to have a firearm.

An immediate shift is unlikely. A gradual erosion is far more likely.

If such a slow shift happens, gun owners will be in a very small mi-nority, so small that any chance of insurrection will be slapped down in a hurry. People will die, yes.

But people are already dying because of government control over lives. A f'r'instance. A majority of the people in the nation want mari-juana decriminalized, but people are still sent to jail for possession.

See Randy Weaver and David Koresh among others. Weaver's wife was killed while she was holding a baby. Her crime? Refusing to surren-der to federal authorities. Weaver's crime? Entrapped (according to the courts) into selling a Class III firearm to an undercover agent. The gun was a short barreled shotgun.

OK, posit a quick repeal of the Second Amendment WITHOUT a paradigm shift in thinking.

You will see mass defections from the military and law enforcement when they are told to go confiscate guns. Most of the people I know on the Thin Blue Line and in the military believe in the right to keep and bear arms.

This will leave a handful of people charged with collecting guns and making arrests. They will now face a larger "enemy" for lack of a better word. They will also face some highly trained opposition. The guys who go into SWAT, SEALS, Rangers, etc are generally the guys and gals who are fervent Second Amendment supporters.

As gun ownership is highest in the South and West, and these legislatures will reject an Amendment repeal, I think a second rebellion is possible. How possible I do not know. Brief aside, if you closely study the history of this nation, a secession attempt was inevitable. If the South hadn't broken away, I believe the West eventually would have.

Anyway, there will be even more bloodshed along the lines of the War of Northern Aggression. I call it the War of Northern Aggression because the Declaration of Independence is either valid document or toilet paper.

"When in the Course of human events it becomes necessary for one people to dissolve the political bands which have connected them with another and to assume among the powers of the earth, the separate and equal station to which the Laws of Nature and of Nature's God entitle them, a decent respect to the opinions of mankind requires that they should declare the causes which impel them to the separation."

http://www.ushistory.org/declaration/document/

As for myself and people who think like me, we will not go gentle into that totalitarian night.

As for myself, if the government decides it wishes to take my guns, I hope the gun grabbing politicians come for them and me and not my friends in the military and law enforcement.

I do not want to shoot anyone. But I will if I have to.

They can have my gun when they pry it from my cold dead fingers. I will take some out before I go.

Cool posters! http://www.a-human-right.com/introduction.html

Making The Point With Different Reasoning

Why should we have guns anyway? Glad you asked.

Anyway, this one is sparked by a FB conversation. I am not providing you the link to that discussion 'cause it is set friends only. Ergo, you couldn't see it. The discussion was over government-provided one-payer, universal health care.

And on that topic, can anyone tell me why John McCain did not go to the VA for treatment?

Yeah.

The point I finally make is - Might makes right. Fair warning, I talk about government-owned guns a lot in this piece, guns aimed at you, me and the guy trying to look into your windows with his binoculars. I'm even gonna prove it.

Also, I may be wrong in what I say below. If I am, please show me. Correct my mistakes. Prove where I went wrong. If you do, I guarantee I will change my view.

BUY THIS INSURANCE OR

WE WILL ARREST YOU

As Muricans, we have the 5-person-ordered right to either purchase health care or go to jail.

Yup. Go to jail.

You say no?

"Because the Constitution permits such a tax, it is not our role to forbid it, or to pass upon its wisdom or fairness," the decision said.

Hey. Don't take my word for it. Here's the entire decision
- http://www.washingtonpost.com/wp-srv/politics/documents/supreme-court-health-care-decision-text.html

It is, according to 5 people, a tax. It is a legal federal tax. Pay it. If you don't pay up you can be arrested. You can go to jail.

Someone is going to point out the Obamacare law does not allow people to be arrested for not having health insurance. The law creates a "fine." Someone will also point out the IRS has no enforcement measures under Obamacare, so if you don't pay the "fine," no worries.

Obamacare didn't need an enforcement clause. The federal income tax codes have plenty of enforcement measures already.

Clear?

http://www.rollingstone.com/music/news/dmx-arrested-for-tax-fraud-allegedly-withheld-17-million-from-irs-w492273

https://www.usnews.com/news/best-states/arkansas/articles/2017-07-11/arkansas-judge-accused-of-not-paying-state-federal-taxes

Al Capone, one of the greatest REAL gangsters of all time, was arrested and sent to jail not for the crimes he was most famous for, but for not paying federal taxes.

Clear?

If you have a job and your employer does not offer health insurance, you have to get it yourself or be found in violation of federal tax law. Never mind if you can't afford it. If you can't afford it and do not get it, you are punished for that.

'Muricans are forced to buy something from a private company or go to jail. No? Try driving your pickup down the road without insurance and get caught by the po-po. You will go to jail.

A FIST IN THE FACE

Those who support OBAMAcare (I use that term because it makes some people mad), generally also support a vast array of government-supplied services.

Full stop. I like government-supplied services. Some of them. I like the ambulance service where I live. I like the fire department. I like the law enforcement agencies. I appreciate the prisons that keep some people off the street. I think prisons should do more to be self-supporting.

Re-engage that transmission and let's resume moving.

Those who support OBAMAcare et al are big on compassion, empathy and the hand of Big Brother reaching toward people.

Depending on how and where you stand that hand is:

• A handout

• A hand up

• A fist to the face

No matter where you stand or how you stand, that fist to the face is for everyone, even those participating in the hands up and hands out. Because in order to give you anything, government first has to take it away.

It does this by way of a gun. I explain below.

The irony of this is, if we refuse to pay, government then converts us to a massive burden on the taxpayers by stripping us of our rights and property, including our right to vote.

And you thought poll taxes were illegal!

CONTRIBUTE OR ELSE

Furthermore, we are forced to support the handout and the hand up, else the fist in the face becomes far more serious. As holding a gun with the barrel shoved up a nostril serious.

https://en.wikipedia.org/wiki/IRS_Criminal_Investigation_Division

Don't like Wikipedia? Ok.

https://www.wsj.com/articles/why-does-the-irs-need-guns-1466117176

And then straight from the gunslingers

https://www.irs.gov/irm/part9/irm_09-001-004.html

Ever been on an IRS raid? I have. I even have the pictures, some of which I published in the newspaper I run, of IRS agents in body armor with firearms standing outside the home they were raiding.

A KINDER AND GENTLER MACHINE GUN IN HAND

Those who argue for government intervention services like to use words like "kindness and compassion," "moral," "ethical" and other high-falutin' words that speak to the nobility of self-sacrifice and helping those in less fortunate situations.

Except they are only looking at one side of that very tangible coin. They completely ignore and most refuse to admit the coin has an obverse.

Ah hell. Might as well spit it out. I am not insulting anyone. I am stating a fact which can be proven empirically. I will even prove it.

These people are delusional, as I prove above and below. Or, hypocrites. Take your pick. Use both.

There is nothing kind... There is nothing compassionate... There is no empathy... It is not "self-sacrifice" to go to a man and take what he owns at gunpoint so it can be given to another. Might makes right. Period. If it did not make right, then people who demand government do this or do that could not make such outrageous statements. They force their beliefs on others at gunpoint. It is what government does - organized violence.

BELIEVE OR ELSE

This reasoning is using violence to enforce a moral code. Period.

These same people who decry the efforts to impose a different moral code - think same-gender marriage which I happen to support because government has no business being involved in marriage - insist it is both right and just to enforce their moral code with violence. Both sides of the government-involved marriage want government guns to enforce their views on same gender marriage.

How is it ethical and moral to use violence to enforce one person's moral code and not another? What makes your code of ethics and morals superior to mine?

The only difference between a robber/burglar/murderer and the government is degree. Period.

When the trigger is pulled, the machine gun does not give a spent primer who is on the receiving end.

YOU ARE VOLUNTEERED

It is, according to the "kind and compassionate" crowd, a matter of charity.

When has charity even been found at the muzzle of a gun?

Charity is doing because you want to. Not because you are forced to.

Those who demand you give and support the use of force to do this often point to the Bible, whether they believe or not. They say Jesus said we are to support the less fortunate.

Yes, we are, according to the Bible. Jesus' instructions are to individuals, not the government. Nowhere does He say it is government's job. No. It is the responsibility of individuals. And, it is a choice individuals get to make.

The difference is the "kind and compassionate" crowd is willing to use force to make you help people. The Good Samaritan is no longer a volunteer but is carrying the pack of the Roman soldier because if he does not, he goes to jail.

https://www.nytimes.com/2017/07/21/us/video-drowning-teens-florida.html

This is horrific? Yup. Is this deplorable? Yup. Is it illegal? Nope. The teens cannot be forced to sacrifice what they have to save another. Except, as noted above and below, they certainly can. It is just a matter of degree.

NB: Since the incident, authorities have charged the teens with failure to report a death. That's like the traffic offense "traveling too fast for conditions." In other words, we believe what you did should be illegal, but it is not, so we're going to come up with something else, make that illegal and charge you with that.

COMPASSIONATE DESTRUCTION

How does ruining someone square with being kind and compassionate? How is it kind and compassionate to throw a person out of his home because he could literally not afford to pay taxes?

http://www.nolo.com/legal-encyclopedia/options-if-you-can-t-pay-the-property-tax-your-home.html

What is kind and compassionate about throwing a person in jail for not paying taxes?

How is it kind and compassionate to take what a person has and throw them in jail because they cannot afford to buy health insurance? How this can be squared with the ethical and moral imperatives of "kindness and compassion" those who push this kind of legislation insist on.

"Because the Constitution permits such a tax, it is not our role to forbid it, or to pass upon its wisdom or fairness," the decision said.

THE WILL OF THE ... SOMETHING

Those who argue for this government intervention into people's lives to "improve them" often fall back on the argument: It is the will of the people.

It ain't.

https://www.dailydot.com/layer8/voter-turnout-2016/

http://thehill.com/homenews/state-watch/324206-new-report-finds-
that-voter-turnout-in-2016-topped-2012

Aaight, so 60 percent of the eligible voters marked their X in the last election.

40 percent never voted. That leaves 60 percent left. Those votes were split. Someone with better math skills than me will have to figure the numbers. Looks like to me, the best a president (pick one, any president) did was maybe 40 percent of the eligible voters.

40 percent ain't the will of anybody except that 40 percent and not even a unanimous will. Your elected reps speak for you. Do you support them? Binary decision. Either they do or they don't. You don't get to pick which decisions you support and which you reject. This is all or nothing because that is way our election system works. The person who takes office is not an amalgam, not a composite. The person in office is going to do exactly what he wants, regardless of your wishes.

It is all or nothing and that's your only choice. Either you support everything your elected rep does, or he does not truly speak for you.

Very very very few people running for office get a clear majority. My rep in the US House ran unopposed. He didn't even manage to get 50 percent of the total eligible votes.

That ain't the will of the people.

THE IMMORAL MINORITY

So let's examine this "majority rule" thing anyway, this idea that so many of the "kind and compassion" crowd talk about.

Majority rule suits them when it goes their way. When it doesn't, "Light the pitchforks, sharpen the torches and call the ACLU cause we're gonna make some lawyers rich!"

If the majority says "This is how it should be" how is it ethical and fair for the minority to say "No, it cannot be that way" and then they get their way? Careful with that sword Damocles!

They (and you, truth be told) do not want majority rule. You want your opinion and ideas to be the law of the land. Hey! Don't look at me that way. I feel the exact same way. The difference is, I'm only willing to resort to violence in defense. The K&C crowd goes on offense with violence.

Here's another hypocrisy - same gender marriage. So many people demand two consenting adults be allowed to decide how to live their lives. Excellent! But these same people have no problem in not even turning around to dictate how those two people must live their lives and expend their resources.

I'm all about "do not harm anyone." The K&C crowd is all about "We're going to harm you to help someone else."

Hypocrite much?

THE DICTATES OF THE FIVE

When groups don't get their way in the ballot box or through legislation, they head to a one-human decision maker - a judge. Eventually, some of these second vacation homes for lawyers reach the US Supreme Court where five people get to decide for the rest of the 300 million people in this nation.

Five people who are not elected. Five people appointed for life or until they decide to retire. They decide and they don't care what you want or think.

Remember OBAMAcare? We were repeatedly told, "It is not a tax."

http://abcnews.go.com/blogs/politics/2012/06/obama-in-2009-its-not-a-tax/

http://www.politico.com/blogs/politico44/2012/06/obama-campaign-its-a-penalty-not-a-tax-127721

https://www.youtube.com/watch?v=tQMkOScXctY

"Because the Constitution permits such a tax, it is not our role to forbid it, or to pass upon its wisdom or fairness," the decision said.

Praise the Supreme Court and pass the ammunition, got some people to ruin because they can't afford to buy something from a private company like we said they have to.

SLAVERY BY ANY OTHER NAME

What we have here is literally slavery by any other name.

If you can be arrested, deprived "of Life, Liberty and the pursuit of Happiness" for failure to share what you have, then how is this different from slavery?

Make note: Failure to share. You are not harming anyone. You are merely minding your own business. Someone comes along and takes what you have.

How is this fair?

SINGLE PAYER SYSTEM

Those who object to buying health insurance from a private company say that's the problem with OBAMAcare. We need a single-payer system, they say.

We have one. It's called the Veterans Administration. Again, can anyone tell me why John McCain didn't go to the VA?

We also have a single-operator system in so many other places. The Post Office, which used to be awesome but today can be counted on to lose important packages.

http://www.thedenverchannel.com/news/front-range/highlands-ranch/highlands-ranch-residents-chronic-lost-mail-issue-needs-fixing

http://www.koaa.com/story/35829567/customers-watch-goes-missing-post-officefails-to-pay-even-though-itwas-insured

http://www.sun-sentinel.com/news/crime/fl-reg-postal-worker-drugs-guilty-20170703-story.html

These are NOT isolated incidents. Talk to people who bulk mail regularly. Talk to the billing department at any utility.

Lots more examples of single-payer systems inefficiencies out there.

For each government efficiency you present, I will present one non-government efficiency and two government inefficiencies.

CHECKING YOUR BALANCE

Supposedly, the system of "checks and balances" is designed to protect the minority against the will of the majority. Those are not my words. Those are the words of a lawyer I personally know who has argued cases before the Supreme Court.

But this system of checks and balances absolutely relies on the support, unwilling or not, of the majority. Don't think so?

As a nation, we've hashed this out with live ammunition, plenty of dead bodies and decades of government intervention. The Civil War, reconstruction and so on, in case you don't get the reference.

But is it really support when the person giving the support is doing it at gunpoint?

Looking for some kindness and compassion. Ain't finding much. Someone help me out.

SPEAKING OF IDIOTS

(MEANING THE AUTHOR OF THIS BOOK)

Quite often when I bring up the ideas of:

• Arresting people for not paying taxes.

• The will of the majority being overruled by the minority.

• How is it kind and compassionate to do all this?

Invectives erupt. Pick your favorite pejorative and it is applied to me and those who think like me.

Or, the subject is changed. A favorite subject change is how those who think like me (please, get professional help if you think like I do) is summed up as "Why won't you agree to help people who need it?"

Please, show me where I said do not help people who need it. Help. I see help as a voluntary action. Help is not showing up at my house with a rock&roll rifle and taking my possessions and putting me in jail.

If your idea of help is taking what someone else has, at the point of a gun, and giving it to someone else, delusional does not begin to describe you.

MONEY AND MOUTH

Ask the K&C crowd how much they do to help the "less fortunate." Direct, hands and wallet-on action. How much? When? Where? I've asked.

"That's why I pay taxes," is the usual response. Very very very few ever make their money follow their mouth. "I pay taxes" is a cop-out anyway. People who say this distance themselves from the dirty work.

Justify it however necessary.

Let's make this personal. If you are one of the K&C crowd, I ask you, how much do you do? What are you willing to do? Give a few cans of food at Thanksgiving and Christmas to a food drive? Drop a dollar in the bucket? Give those old, stained, torn, stretched and worn out clothes to a thrift shop?

Ain't you just the heart of charity.

You are fully within your rights to ask to what I do. Words are worthless. Come spend a month with me and see for yourself. See for yourself if I walk the same as I talk. Bring some clothes that you can get bloody. Yes. Real hemoglobin. If you are gonna hang with me, you are gonna do as I do.

THE SYSTEM

A few people say "This is the system we have."

Yeah. It is. I am working within the legal framework of that system to change it. So are they. Hopefully, so are you.

And now for a bad joke.

Brunhilda: Did you know bull fighting is the most popular sport in South America?

Clothilda: That's revolting!

Brunhilda: No, that's the second favorite sport.

Unfortunately, the rumblings you now feel may be the precursor to a far more physical change. Domestic terrorists are not killing people because the terrorists had a bad day. They see the killing as the only way to effect the change they want to see.

One man is a terrorist bent on mayhem and destruction. 1 million men are an army determined to enforce the will of the people and bring peace by whatever means necessary.

One man's terrorist is another man's freedom fighter.

THE GREATER EVIL

A common argument by those supporting OBAMAcare is 1) "it is for the greater good." and 2) They admit "some people will fall through the cracks."

1) HELL NO in flaming letters tall enough to be read from orbit.

"The greater good" is the universal justification for the most incredible atrocities humans inflict on humans. The Inquisitions tortured people for their greater good.

"He has refused his Assent to Laws, the most wholesome and necessary for the public good." What was that "wholesome and necessary" stuff? How about protection from ,"the merciless Indian Savages whose known rule of warfare, is an undistinguished destruction of all ages, sexes and conditions. This "wholesome and necessary" stuff led to genocide.

http://www.cs.virginia.edu/~evans/cs655/readings/declaration.html

How about Mao Tse Tung? "Over the next few years, Mao Tse-tung instituted sweeping land reform, sometimes through persuasion and other times through coercion, using violence and terror when he deemed it necessary." https://www.biography.com/people/mao-tse-tung-9398142

Pol Pot. "During that time, about 1.5 million Cambodians out of a total population of 7 to 8 million died of starvation, execution, disease or overwork. Some estimates place the death toll even higher. One detention center, S-21, was so notorious that only seven of the roughly 20,000 people imprisoned there are known to have survived." http://www.history.com/topics/pol-pot

Stalin. "Millions of farmers refused to cooperate with Stalin's orders and were shot or exiled as punishment. The forced collectivization also led to widespread famine across the Soviet Union that killed millions."

http://www.history.com/topics/joseph-stalin

Can't happen here? A president killed US citizens without giving them the due process rights enshrined in the Constitution.

http://www.politifact.com/texas/statements/2014/mar/19/kesha-rogers/four-us-citizens-killed-obama-drone-strikes-3-were/

Foreign soil you say?

http://www.nytimes.com/1985/05/14/us/police-drop-bomb-on-radi-cals-home-in-philadelphia.html?pagewanted=all

The peace prize winning president took us to war (war is defined as a military attack on a nation) into more countries than anyone else. But it was for the greater good.

http://www.latimes.com/projects/la-na-pol-obama-at-war/

Every war fought is done for "the greater good." The exact phrasing varies. The justification is exactly the same.

2) Yep. People fall through the cracks. From time immemorial, the government solution for these people is to ignore where possible, kill where ignoring them does not work and make a great show of trying to do right by these people while making life worse for them.

A terrorist by any other name...

PAGING CLARA PELLER

Here's a beef ... no. Here's an entire Montana herd worth of cows I have with this. Let's make this personal.

You, you who call for kindness and compassion and insist on taking what belongs to me to make this happen. You are ... sigh. No help for it.

You are a coward.

The guy who pulls a knife and takes a wallet from someone on the street has far more courage and conviction than you do. He is willing to do the deed himself. He is willing to put his life on the line for what he wants.

You, nah. You hide behind such things as "the law" and the "will of the people" and hire other people to go out with guns to enforce your directives. You stand well-removed from the potential reality of lethal violence and let others do it because you simply don't have the courage to do it yourself. Proof below.

CALL ME OUT

Yeah. You read that right. Call me out. Stand up. HUMAN UP. Do the deed yourself.

Come to my house and YOU collect what you believe I owe society. You do it. Do not depend on the hired employee to do the dirty work of your collections.

Come on.

Figured as much.

COME SEE THE VIOLENCE

A very few of the "kind and compassionate" crowd are willing to admit to the violence inherent in the system. They even admit they do not like it. They are not forthcoming with alternatives. They cannot grasp alternatives, even when the alternatives are actually working right now.

https://www.charitynavigator.org/

The extremely rare person who is in the "K&C" crowd and admits these outfits do an awesome job will also say, "They don't do enough so we must have government."

And there is the violence inherent in the system. When you go from "should" to "must", then a gun barrel is shoved up someone's nostril. In the case of "government" demanding it, the nation takes the gun and shoves it up the collective nostril of the nation.

Some us are trying to put the gun down. Some are grasping it harder.

MIGHT MAKES RIGHT

What this all comes down to is - Might makes right.

You do not have to agree. Reality is under no obligation to conform itself to your expectations and if the truth hurts, yer living wrong.

Might makes right. If enough people agree, then it becomes the right thing to do. The US Constitution SPECIFICALLY says if enough people agree, it is the right thing to do. Yes it does. Look it up. SCOTUS says the same thing. Yes hunh. Look at the decision on pornography.

What that reasoning does is kill people because they want to be in charge of what they have. Not harming anyone. But they are killed because you say they have to die because they will not surrender what they have or do what you say they have to do.

http://abcnews.go.com/US/story?id=95475

http://www.cbsnews.com/news/botched-atlanta-drug-raid-killed-92-year-old-woman-family-awarded-49-million/

http://www.dispatch.com/content/stories/local/2013/12/13/woman-accidentally-shot-by-ross-county-deputies-in-raid.html

http://www.pennlive.com/midstate/index.ssf/2012/08/ruby_ridge_20_years_later.html

http://www.ohiohistorycentral.org/w/Kent_State_Shootings

And again - http://www.nytimes.com/1985/05/14/us/police-drop-bomb-on-radicals-home-in-philadelphia.html

I wanna see you make the dead guy understand why he had to be killed for doing nothing more than wanting to run his own life. Explain, so that he understands, that you are sorry he fell through the cracks. Tell him, so he can understand, why it was necessary for him to die so someone else could be helped.

Send me the video of your explanation, please. I'll take a transcript too, but I want to see the reaction of the dead guy.

Guns Regulated Like Vehicles? Yes Please.

People who don't know any better keep saying we need to regulate guns like vehicles. People who don't know any better fly into a rage over this idea.

Yes. Regulate guns like vehicles. Please. Can we do that immediately?

Let's put a critical eye on this detail and lemme show you why people who truly believe that either do not know what they are talking about or they are people who truly understand the 2nd Amendment.

Sometimes I provide examples. Sometimes I do not, but I will if you ask. Fair warning - this is long and may get longer as I remember things. I am trying to be comprehensive.

If I have made a mistake, or left something out, tell me. I will edit and revise. And I have revised a few times as I remember stuff. Interesting, no one from the gun control lobby has mentioned any oversights.

Points are listed at random.

Start here-

OPERATION

Vehicles

Every state grants exceptions for operating vehicles on public roads, NO LICENSE NEEDED. Look. It. Up. Tractors and combines are included in the definition of a vehicle. More definition follows. You may disagree with the definition of vehicle here, in which case you are wrong. Seriously. I am well-tired of people who cannot read their local, state and federal laws regarding the definition of vehicle and operation thereof. If you intend to argue this point, I ~~probably~~ will block you. Read. The. Law.

Ag vehicles, which include cropdusters, are capable of more than 100 miles an hour and have more horsepower than anything Detroit produces these days. With a wagon on the back, think hayride, they can haul as many people as a school bus.

I checked about dozen states. For the operation of ag vehicles on public roads:

- No age limit

- No vehicle registration

- No insurance

Further, many communities allow golf carts on public roads. My community does. No license needed. My community does have an insurance requirement and an age limit. Other golf cart communities do not.

A public license is not needed to drive vehicles on private property. Insurance is not needed.

Operating a vehicle on a public road is legal.

Follow the rules of the road, which are pretty uniform from state to state.

Driving toward someone is legal. Running them over is not.

States set speed limits. There is no firearm equivalent, unless you refer to rate of fire which is governed by federal law.

Law enforcement must have a warrant or have a reasonable belief that a crime is being committed to go onto private property to check a vehicle.

Seat belt use is a state-level requirement. There is no firearm equivalent.

Your state requirements may vary.

Firearms

Operating a firearm on a public road is generally illegal. Some Western states allow hunting from the road. Restrictions apply and vary by state.

In general, just shooting from a public road is not permitted.

Pointing a gun down the road just to do it is illegal.

Firing a gun across lanes of traffic is illegal.

Pointing a gun at someone is questionable. Shooting at someone, regardless of impact, is illegal unless in self-defense. In some states, lethal use of a firearm even in self-defense can result in criminal charges.

Some states actually require you to retreat in the face of lethal threats. Not kidding. There is no vehicular equivalent. Get you some -

http://criminal.findlaw.com/criminal-law-basics/states-that-have-stand-your-ground-laws.html

Minors may operate firearms when under supervision of an adult.

Discharging a firearm in the city limits, except under highly specific circumstances, is generally illegal.

Law enforcement can go onto private property to check a firearm without suspecting illegal activity and without a warrant.

OPERATING RESTRICTIONS

In addition to the restrictions mentioned above, I have one more to add.

The breathalyzer for a vehicle. This is also called an ignition inter-lock. https://dui.drivinglaws.org/interlock.php

Of course, this is easy to defeat. Unhook the thing. However, it is court-required in some cases.

Someone is going to add, as this guy at Forbes did, this is an invalid argument.

https://www.forbes.com/sites/joshmax/2017/10/10/comparing-gun-carnage-with-auto-deaths-is-a-flawed-argument/#714cc6a1483e

Really?

When a person dies by the hand of another human being, does it really matter HOW they died, unless it is euthanasia which is a whole 'other topic? Is a cold-blooded murder with a pistol any different than someone burning to death in a crash caused by a DUI driver?

http://abc7.com/traffic/3-killed-dui-suspect-arrested-after-oc-crash/3277582/

So how many people die in DUI v. guns anyway? This site -

http://www.romans322.com/daily-death-rate-statistics.php -

purports to keep track. As of this writing, DUI deaths were 3:1 compared to gun deaths.

The CDC says gun deaths and vehicle deaths are a dead (AR HAR HAR) heat. This of course includes suicide and accidental death.

https://www.cdc.gov/nchs/fastats/injury.htm

The National Highway Transportation and Safety Administration has plenty of stats on vehicle deaths.

https://crashstats.nhtsa.dot.gov/Api/Public/ViewPublication/811016

Newsweek whines that "The consequences for driving while intoxicated are strict: All 50 states have implemented a legal limit of .08 percent blood alcohol concentration for drivers. People under 21 face zero-tolerance policies nationwide, and individual states have felony driving-under-the-influence laws."

http://www.newsweek.com/texas-church-shooting-gun-violence-statistics-702546

As if the laws regarding murder are a trifle.

Solution? Breathalyzer in ALL VEHICLES. Disconnect the device, jail time to be determined but I suggest along the same lines as the sentence for armed robbery.

So what about killing someone while drunk? What's the penalty? By and large the charge is manslaughter. Manslaughter means killing someone without malice aforethought, by accident or under circumstances that are not murder. A murder charge in a DUI is very rare.

Ahem.

Talk to someone who lost a mom, dad, brother or sister or a CHILD to a DUI driver and ask them what the charge should be.

DUI manslaughter penalties are widely disparate. In some states, you can get two years. Some up to 15.

For murder? How about the death penalty for the max sentence.

And juuuuust in case you thought it was safe to climb on a high horse and whine at me:

"Sentences are longest in murder types where apprehension rates are low, and where deterrence elasticities appear to be high. However, sentences respond to victim characteristics in a way that is hard to reconcile with optimal punishment. In particular, victim characteristics are important determinants of sentencing among vehicular homicides, where victims are basically random and where the optimal punishment model predicts that victim characteristics should be ignored. Among vehicular homicides, drivers who kill women get 56 percent longer sentences. Drivers who kill blacks get 53 percent shorter sentences." Get you some - http://www.nber.org/papers/w7676

BANNED

Vehicles

I am not aware of any kind of vehicle banned by a state. It may exist. I don't know about it. The federal government bans vehicles. NB: I cannot swear this website is accurate. Some of the "banned" vehicles and the reasons given appear to conflict with vehicles already on the road in the US. I also believe this list is not complete; other vehicles may be banned by the US.

http://www.odometer.com/rides/33511/14-vehicles-that-arent-allowed-in-to-the-united-states/

Federal import rules

https://icsw.nhtsa.gov/cars/rules/import/FMVSS/

Firearms

Several states outright ban certain categories of firearms except for law enforcement use. Get some -

https://www.nraila.org/gun-laws/state-gun-laws/

This link runs you to the actual state law, not NRA hype.

The federal government has banned a bunch.

https://www.nraila.org/articles/20140717/obama-administration-bans-import-of-popular-russian-firearms

http://warisboring.com/trump-expands-on-what-obama-started-banning-russian-rifle-imports/

http://www.nytimes.com/1989/07/08/us/import-ban-on-assault-rifles-becomes-permanent.html

http://www.wideopenspaces.com/5-banned-guns-banned-u-s-import/

This is in addition to the select-fire manufacturing restriction passed during the Reagan era.

OWNERSHIP

Vehicle

Anyone can legally own a vehicle, at least under federal law. State law may say differently. The only knot in this particular rope is the age of the owner. Under federal and state law, a minor cannot enter into a legal contract. So, is owning a vehicle a legal contract? If the vehicle needs to be financed, yes. If the vehicle is bought outright or a gift, no. Minors buy things in stores all the time. No contract needed.

https://www.autobytel.com/car-ownership/maintenance-repair/at-what-age-can-you-purchase-a-car-104037/

Vehicles may be given outright to minors. The late Dr. Penn White gave my son Jesse an MG Midget. Jesse was in elementary school at the time.

A person convicted of a felony may legally own a vehicle. A person convicted of multiple DUI infractions may own a vehicle.

Not aware of any ownership restrictions in any state for vehicles, up to and including decommissioned tanks.

Vehicles may be given as gift without restriction.

No limit on the number of vehicles that may be owned.

No state has a waiting period for purchasing a vehicle

The Constitution does not guarantee the right to own a vehicle.

Firearm

To legally own certain classes of firearm, a person must be at least 18 under federal law. That is for long guns. The age is 21 for handguns.

Several states outright ban certain categories of firearms except for law enforcement use.

Firearms may be gifted, provided the receiver is legally allowed to own the firearm under state and federal law.

No limit on the number of firearms that may be owned. Possession of more than a certain amount of a single caliber or gauge of ammunition requires a federal arsenal permit.

A person convicted of a felony may not legally own a firearm. A person committed to a mental institution may not legally own a firearm. A person convicted of assault may not own a firearm. The list goes on.

Get some - https://www.atf.gov/firearms/identify-prohibited-persons

Some states impose a waiting limit on buying a firearm.

When buying a firearm from a licensed dealer, the BATFE may impose a 3-day waiting period with no explanation. At the end of the period, the BATFE may say no sale, sale approved, or sale to be determined by the license holder. There is no vehicle equivalent.

The Constitution backed up by a Supreme Court decision, says owning a firearm is a Constitutional right.

http://lawcenter.giffords.org/gun-laws/policy-areas/who-can-have-a-gun/minimum-age/#federal

Three significant pieces of legislation also govern certain kinds of firearms. There is no vehicle equivalent.

https://www.atf.gov/rules-and-regulations/national-firearms-act

PURCHASE

Vehicle

Got money? Buy it.

Those on the left say that if you are in business, you must do business with anyone who has money. Bake a cake, in other words.

Prohibiting someone from legally owning a vehicle requires an order from a judge.

Sales from a dealer are subject to local sales tax and possibly property taxes and possibly local registration requirements. I say possibly because collector vehicles may not be registered in some places. Also, in some states the purchase of ag vehicles is exempt from sales tax.

Purchase of new vehicles with certain engine types may allow the owner an income tax break.

https://ttlc.intuit.com/questions/2588802-how-to-claim-a-new-car-on-your-taxes

Anyone may cross a state line and buy a vehicle in a state where they do not live.

Firearm

Buying from a dealer requires either a federal background check OR a state-approved firearms license. Regardless, federal paperwork must be filled out when buying from a dealer.

Federal regulations allow require a firearms dealer to refuse a sale if he believes the buyer should not have the firearm EVEN IF THE BUYER PASSES THE FEDERAL BACKGROUND CHECK. A firearms dealer may refuse to sell a firearm without giving a reason. Federal regulation.

Private sales may or may not require background checks, depending on state law. Regardless, sale of a firearm to someone legally prohibited from owning a firearm is a federal offense.

Prohibiting someone from owning a firearm may require an order from a judge, i.e. criminal conviction, judged mentally incompetent, etc. Preventing someone over 21 from legally owning a firearm may not require a judge's order, i.e. being under psyche-type care.

Sales from a dealer are subject to the federal Pittman-Robertson act taxes, local sales taxes and possibly local registration requirements.

https://www.fws.gov/laws/lawsdigest/fawild.html

When buying a firearm in another state, only long guns may be purchased by a non-resident, subject to everything else listed above and below. Handgun purchases are only allowed within the state of residence. This is a federal regulation and has no vehicle equivalent.

One firearm may be purchased per year and deducted from federal taxes, if the firearm is used in a business. Farming allows this for crop predation control. Think hunting wild hogs to save the peanuts.

I have a 3/4 inch thick book from the BATF giving me the regulations on the sale of firearms. I doubt the vehicle industry has the same.

CLASSES

Vehicles

Vehicles are grouped into classes. Ag. Commercial transport (semi). Commercial person transport (bus, limo). Recreational. Racing/Professional sport. Passenger/Private. Aquatic. Air. AutoCycle (in some states). Motorcycle. Industrial (in some states). Driving SOME of these vehicles requires a license. Some require an advanced or special license.

Firearms

Firearms are in classes.

Some are not regulated. Airguns are not considered firearms, depending on the use and state regulations. Antique meaning made before 1898. Obsolete, meaning ammo for the firearm is no longer available. Muzzleloader, meaning it must be loaded from the muzzle and cannot use modern smokeless powder; can be handgun or long gun. (Savage and Daisy experienced this requirement and those guns are now collector's items, commanding a serious price.) Anyone can buy and own these, subject to state law. No license needed to buy, own or sell. Age requirement is a gray area.

HOWEVER - The definition of "weapon" is highly subjective and may include any of the above. Take a blacktopped pistol to rob a bank, and you are guilty of armed robbery. Same with an airgun. There is no vehicle equivalent.

Curio & Relic, meaning 40 years old or older or special designation into this category by the BATFE. BATFE has a special firearms license for this category allowing the holder to buy and sell guns in this group across state lines.

Long guns are a category. Think shotgun and rifle. Long gun barrel length is federally regulated to a minimum.

Handguns are a category. Think Dirty Harry's revolver. Handgun barrel length is federally regulated to a maximum.

A new class of short-barreled shotgun, with a pistol grip, was recently added to the categories. These firearms must still maintain a minimum length. Addition of a shoulder stock, even once, moves these guns into the Tax Stamp short barreled firearm category.

Tax Stamp required firearms are short-barreled long guns (any other weapon). Fully automatic (select-fire). Destructive Devices (DD), items having a bore of more than a half-inch and generally recognized as not having any sporting use.

Sporting use means 10 and 8 gauge shotguns (which would otherwise be a DD) are sporting arms despite the bore size. Other examples are the 577 Tyrannosaur, the 600 and 700 Nitro Express double rifles, the 4-bore and the 2-bore.

Industrial application. These firearms are special use and special manufacture. They are not used for hunting, sporting, training or law enforcement purposes. (Nor would you want to for that matter.) They are found in very specific factories and coal-burning power plants where they are used to remove "eyebrows" from drums and boilers. They could fall under the tax-stamp requirement under a strict interpretation of the law, but they are not placed there. As best I know, Remington and Winchester are the sole US manufacturers of these firearms.

Railguns are not regulated in any fashion I'm aware of. There is no vehicle equivalent. Still, use one in the commission of a crime, and you will be charged with using a "weapon."

LICENSE

Vehicle

A driver's license from any state or territory is valid in any other state or territory. 16 is the minimum age to receive a license. A learner's permit is available at 15. There is no minimum age needed to obtain a private pilot's license.

Every state is a "shall issue" for driver's licenses. Pass the test, get a license. You cannot be denied unless your license is suspended for some infraction. Licensing requirements vary by state.

Once you get a license in one state, you can move to another state and get the same license there without testing.

A license is not required to own a vehicle.

Firearm

A weapons permit is only valid in the state of issue and in states with a reciprocal agreement. A Georgia driver's license is valid in any US state or territory. A Georgia firearms permit is only valid in the Peach State and in states with a reciprocity agreement.

Get some - https://www.usacarry.com/concealed_carry_permit_reci-
procity_maps.html

Most states with a carry license have a minimum age of 21 for the permit. Getting a permit in some states requires some training.

Some states are "shall issue." Some states are "may issue." May issue means you can be denied a license for any reason or no reason. Some states are "open carry" meaning no license is required.

Some states do not require any training for a firearms license.

A firearms license will not automatically transfer to another state. You must meet that state's requirements.

https://www.thetrace.org/2016/02/live-fire-training-not-mandatory-
concealed-carry-permits/

A license is not required to own a gun.

Tax Stamp

It is not a license, but rather a federal tax stamp. The stamp is needed to legally own a DD, short barrel firearm or select-fire gun in every state and territory This paperwork must be in possession of the person who has the tax stamp weapon in every state and territory.

https://www.atf.gov/qa-category/national-firearms-act-nfa

Some states do not allow certain tax-stamp firearms.

A tax-stamp firearm also requires approval from a local law enforce-ment agency head. This permission may be denied with no reason given.

A National Firearms Act (NFA) trust may be created to "own" a Tax Stamp firearm or accessory. Local law enforcement permission is not re-quired. Other requirements remain. Other "users" may be added to this trust, provided the person is eligible to legally use a firearm. No checks are required to add people.

MOVING

Vehicle

You can drive any vehicle across state lines, provided it meets the local and state road requirements for being on the road. It may mean headlights, brake lights and turn signals, safety belts, insurance, registration and a license. As noted above, these items are not always required.

Firearm

You must meet the state and local regulations, which vary widely. New York prohibits magazines above a certain capacity. New York also requires firearms be carried in a separate locked container from ammunition. Other states vary in transportation requirements.

Transporting a tax stamp weapon (think full auto) means the person with the weapon and the tax stamp must alert authorities that the weapon is crossing state lines. Some states prohibit certain tax stamp firearms, so transporting it across a state line is illegal even if you call ahead.

SUPPLIES

Vehicle

Dispensing gasoline must be overseen by someone with a driver's license or over 18. This is rarely enforced in my opinion as young'uns are routinely seen buying gas in gas cans for lawnmowers & so forth.

Parts may be purchased by anyone with money.

Oil, filters, transmission fluid, etc. may be purchased by anyone with money.

Firearm

Purchasing ammo requires the person to be at least 18 or 21 depending on the ammo. Strictly handgun ammo, the buyer must be 21. If the ammo can be handgun or long gun, the seller has to be sure the person buying will use it in a long gun if the buyer is under 21.

Reloading supplies may be purchased by anyone.

RESTRICTIONS

Vehicle

Some roads and bridges in every state are weight-restricted.

Some states and cities have emissions requirements for vehicles.

Height requirements are set by state law.

https://ops.fhwa.dot.gov/freight/publications/size_regs_final_rpt/

Firearm

Restrictions noted throughout this article.

LOCATION

Vehicles

Vehicles may be parked on public property, school grounds, state and federal enclaves in marked places and sometimes unmarked places. Vehicles may be taken into buildings on these properties.

Businesses are free to restrict vehicle possession and use on their grounds.

Age restrictions are possible, but unusual unless linked directly to the age needed for the license (21 for CDL.)

Firearms

Firearms may not be taken into buildings on these properties. Some exceptions are for organized and coached sporting events. Shotgun tournaments hosted by the 4-H is an example, but the firearms are closely monitored and the person must adhere to a volume of safety regulations.

A person over 18 must be in attendance for a firearm to be legally allowed on school grounds even for an organized event.

Businesses are free to restrict firearm possession and use on their grounds.

MISCELLANEOUS LAWS

Commission of a Crime

Vehicle

Possession of a vehicle during the commission of a crime is not an additional charge in most states. Using the vehicle to actually commit the crime (run over someone) may be different. Your state regs may vary.

Firearm

Possession of a firearm during the commission of a crime is an additional charge in every state. Possession of a firearm by a convicted felon during commission of a crime is an additional charge in every state.

Weight

Vehicle

Vehicle size is governed by weight, with a maximum set under state and federal law. Exceptions many be granted by seeking special permission. There is no firearm equivalent.

Misuse

Vehicle

Misuse of a vehicle ranges from a civil offense to a federal capital punishment eligible crime.

Firearm

Misuse of a firearm is a crime ranging from a misdemeanor to a federal capital punishment eligible crime.

Hunting

Vehicle

Some states allow hunting from a vehicle. Regs vary by state.

Firearm

All states have restrictions on firearm types, caliber and shot size for hunting.

Rifling

Except in the new category of shotgun with has a minimum length, barrels shorter than certain length must have rifling grooves. To do otherwise creates a short-barreled gun subject to the Tax Stamp. There is no vehicle equivalent.

HazMat

Vehicle

Hazardous material transport applies to certain items hauled in vehicles, including ammunition primer and powder. It also applies to acids, fuels and etc. Aside from an upper gross vehicle weight limit, there is no limit to how much fuel a vehicle may transport without needing a HazMat permit. This may appear to be a contradiction on fuel, but it is not. Semis routinely haul hundreds of pounds of fuel to engine consumption, no permit needed. Hauling it as cargo is hazmat.

Firearm

HazMat applies to transport of ammo, powder and primers over a certain weight, under 10 pounds as I remember, for private transport. HazMat applies to any commercial transport of said items. Amount of ammunition over a certain amount is subject to federal regulation.

Fuel

Vehicle

Fuel must be stored in approved containers. Storing fuel in glass jars is considered construction of a Destructive Device and subject to a federal Tax Stamp.

Firearms

Powder may be stored in glass jars. Powder stored in pipes and other improvised explosive devices determined by an investigating officer may be considered Destructive Devices and subject to the federal Tax Stamp.

COMMERCIAL SALES

Vehicle

To get a vehicle sales license, some states require classes, insurance and a regular license fee. This varies by state. Most cities also require a business license for the dealer.

Firearm

To get a federal firearms license, the person must:

- Be fingerprinted.

- Undergo an extensive background check, much more thorough than the check needed to buy a firearm.

- Have the premises where the firearms are sold inspected. Inspections may be done annually.

- Prove he wants the license to make money (Yes. This is a federal requirement.)

- Have a meeting with a BATFE agent to discuss the application (for a commercial dealer or higher license. Not needed for Curio & Relict)

- Pay the license fee each year or every three years, depending on the license.

- Keep records for 20 years of every transaction.

- Prove firearms can be stored in a safe location.

- Report any theft of a firearm to the BATFE within 24 hours.

- Submit reports (depending on license) on all firearms sales to local law enforcement regularly (depending on local regs).

- Have a physical location.

- Have the property zoned for commercial firearms sales (C&R excepted).

- Specify which license is requested. BATFE has a bunch. It ranges from the C&R to the destructive device construction and import license.

- A business license.

Get some - https://www.atf.gov/qa-category/licenses-and-permits

ACCESSORIES

Vehicle

Vehicle accessories are limited. Blue lights are restricted to law enforcement use and special permit.

Flashing lights may be restricted by state or local law.

Vehicle height is restricted by local law in some places.

Window tint is restricted in some states.

Other accessories may be limited by local or state law.

Fuel composition is governed by state and federal law. There is no exact parallel to firearms.

Firearm

Some states restrict magazine capacity.

Some states restrict stocks - nothing collapsible, sliding wire -rame, front grips, etc.

Certain projectiles are illegal under federal law. There is no exact parallel to vehicles.

Changing barrels on the firearm may be federally illegal, depending on the configuration of the firearm and the length of the barrel and rifling in the barrel, without a Tax Stamp.

Federal law specifies what part of a firearm is the actual "gun." Must meet federal requirements to own this. Other parts may be purchased by anyone. Possession of certain parts of a firearm, not the "gun" is illegal without a Tax Stamp.

SOUND

Vehicle

Some states ban vehicles without mufflers. Some states put decibel limits on motorcycles. No jake brakes in some localities.

https://www.jacobsvehiclesystems.com/parts-service-support/how-an-engine-brake-works/

Firearm

Some states and communities outright ban suppressors. Some restrict them. Regardless, it requires a federal Tax Stamp for each suppressor.

REGISTRATION

Vehicle

Vehicle registration varies by state and vehicle. Sometimes required, sometimes not.

Firearm

Registration varies by state and firearm. Sometimes required, mostly not.

KITS

Vehicle

Anyone can buy a kit vehicle and put it together. Registration requirement varies by state. The vehicle may be sold to anyone.

Inspection often required in order to get registration and tags.

Once made, can be sold to anyone.

Firearm

Anyone can buy an unrestricted firearm kit, blacktopped for instance, and put it together.

Other classes are subject to federal firearm ownership restrictions. Construction and possession is illegal as noted above.

Sale of kit firearms, which are subject to federal regulation is generally prohibited, unless it is done through a dealer. If you make your own centerfire or rimfire firearm you do not need to put a serial number on it. This is recommended. If no serial number, you cannot sell this firearm, but may leave it to someone in your will.

No one, excepting someone with a Class III or higher manufacturer's permit, may make a DD or select-fire firearm. Select-fire may only be sold to law enforcement or kept as a demonstration model. If the Class III or higher license is ever surrendered or not renewed, any display firearm must be turned into the BATFE.

No inspection requirements.

The "80 percent" rule allows anyone to buy a block that needs machining work to become a completed firearm. This is a precision operation and well beyond the capabilities of most people without a CNC machine. CNC devices are thousands to hundreds of thousands of dollars. The block has to be no more than 80 percent complete. If the person is prohibited from owning a firearm, completing the block to make it into a firearm is a federal crime.

INSTRUCTOR

Vehicle

Depending on the kind of instruction, requirements vary. Class requirements vary.

Firearm

Depending on kind of instruction, requirements vary, but at minimum require a background check and be legally allowed to own a firearm as well as tax certifying classes by a certifying agency.

MANUFACTURE & REPAIR

Vehicle

Federal law oversees the license for manufacturing of commercial vehicles. It has three levels. 1) A custom shop that turns out a few vehicles a year. Think racing shop. No license needed. 2) Small manufacturer. I forget the number made in a year before this requirement kicks in. 3) Mass market. Ford, Chrysler, GMC, etc.

Repair shops generally need a local business license. They may be subject to additional taxes and laws such as workman's comp and unemployment insurance.

Any repair shop may repair any vehicle, if the shop is capable. In general, no specific license is required to be a mechanic. State laws may vary. No license is needed to send a vehicle across a state line for repair. Certifications are available.

Certain parts on vehicles may not be repaired by the owner, under the federal Digital Millennium Copyright Act (DCMA); this affects the software and electronic components used by the software. Only licensed shops may effect the repair. There is no firearm equivalent.

Manufacture of a kit vehicle or a restoration does not require registration. Manufacture for commercial sale requires federal registration of some sort of identification number, be that a VIN or engine number.

Federal and local regulations govern emissions.

https://www.nhtsa.gov/laws-regulations

Firearm

The manufacture of 1 firearm for commercial sale requires a federal gun manufacturing license. BATFE recently ruled that making some modifications to firearms parts, threading a barrel for instance for commercial sale, also requires a federal firearms license.

Gunsmith shops generally need a local business license. They may be subject to additional taxes and laws such as workman's comp and unemployment insurance.

Working on Class III or other Tax Stamp firearms requires the gunsmith to hold the necessary federal licenses to possess and work on such items. Gunsmiths are not required to have a federal firearms license, but it is recommended. If the gun passes over a state line to the smith direct, a license is required. Certifications are available.

The owner may repair any part of his firearm without license or approval, unless the firearm requires software and electronic parts governed by software, in which case the federal DMCA applies. If that happens, only a licensed shop may effect repairs.

Manufacture of a firearm for private use and not for sale under any circumstances does not require registration. The maker still must be allowed to own the firearm under local, state and federal law. Manufacture for commercial sale requires federal registration of the serial number.

Select-fire firearms may not be manufactured by an individual without the appropriate federal licenses. Other Tax Stamp weapons may be legally manufactured by an individual after paying the Tax Stamp and received BATFE approval.

Federal law requires the use of non-toxic (steel, bismuth, tungsten) shot for hunting waterfowl. California has non-lead hunting bullet requirements.

https://www.atf.gov/resource-center/docs/atf-p-5300-4pdf/download

A few words to 'splain

To help some of you better understand this, a few words to 'splain the whats, whys and wherefores of this book.

I own a gun - I carry a gun because I have been threatened with physical violence and attacked more than once. I have survived an assassination attempt. I carry a gun because 911 is government-sponsored dial-a-prayer (no offense to the GREAT people working those places). The last time I called 911 for police (attempted assassination), it was slightly more than two minutes before they arrived. I have a gun because I cannot afford 24/7 bodyguards.

I believe I have the right to defend myself - If you attack me, I have the right to respond. Whether or not I respond is up to me and the amount of response I give should be proportional to the attack levied. You have the same rights.

Just because I believe it, doesn't make it right, the truth or something that needs to be - The same applies to you. If you won't force your beliefs on me, I won't force mine on you. I'll be glad to discuss them any time you wish and will extend the same courtesy to you, quid pro quo.

I believe in God - I believe in Jesus and I believe that the modern translations of the Bible, including the KJV, are not perfect but do contain plenty of wisdom and are excellent guides for living for everyone, whether they are Christian or not.

I believe in tithing - I do, really. But I also do not believe in supporting a bloated and parasitic church hierarchy. I believe in a supporting a local church which works in its community, does community outreach and genuinely tries to be connected to people. You cannot force people to return that connection. A church does not need a million dollar building and does not need to send missionaries overseas when people in the church's community are hurting and hungry and in need.

Jesus didn't turn the water into Tang - Look it up.

I believe in second chances - I have been given second chances beyond counting.

I believe in forgiveness - This does not contradict with my belief of accountability.

I believe in a hand up not a hand out - I will help anyone who is trying for as long and as much as I can. I will not help people who are just looking for a free ride.

If I choose to help someone, that's my business - What I do with what is mine is no concern of yours unless you can prove it is harming you. At the same time, no one has the right to force me to help someone.

I believe in accepting the consequences for actions - If you do it, you are responsible. Don't look to place the blame on someone else. Shut up, suck it up and move on. If you need help, and are willing to admit where the real fault lies, I'm there for you. If you are interested in casting blame, go away.

Government cannot give unless it first takes - Government does not manufacture, produce or generate anything without first restricting the rights of others to do the same thing. In some cases this is necessary. In some cases this is not.

If I earn it, it is mine - Just because I have more than you doesn't mean you have the right to take it, and that includes by government fiat. Just because I have less than you doesn't give me the right to take it from you, even by government fiat.

I believe in very limited taxes - Some government functions are necessary. Police, Fire, National defense, a national money system, courts.

I believe in free speech - Say on Say on. I may not agree with what you say, but I will defend to my death your right to say it, if necessary. Offensive speech is important and should be said because if you look long enough and hard enough, you will find SOMEONE to take offense to anything which is said. This book is certainly proof.

I like and do not like reality - It can be painful. It can hurt. But I'd rather deal with what is real than put on rose-colored glasses and ignore the empirical evidence.

I can be convinced otherwise if you have cogent, sound, reasoned and decent information. My mind is suspect to change with new evidence. Blind adherence to any dogma is unhealthy. You can't prove anything with a negative.

Music, good music, says far more than the notes and words - I don't care what the music is. Classical, Jazz, Rock, Pop, Southern Fried Rock, Metal, Gospel, Rap. Pick a genre. There is a bunch junk in all the genres too. The trick is to find what's worthwhile and listen to it and throw the rest in a compost heap.

I believe in voter-driven term limits for elected officials - In other words vote. I do not want nor need a law telling me I can't vote for someone. If you don't like what the person is doing, vote for someone else. If you like what the person is doing vote for 'em. Voters have the ability to throw anyone out of office at any time. We just have to be willing to do that.

I believe ignorance is curable - Ignorance is simply a lack of knowledge. Stupidity, on the other hand, is a rejection of knowledge and can't be cure, only eliminated.

Children should be cherished - Feed them. Love them. Respect them. Teach them. Be there for them. You do not need money to be a good parent. You don't have to be biologically related to be a good parent. You don't even have to be a parent.

Loud pipes save lives - Purple Haze has a kickin' set of pipes. Yes, I know it annoys some people, but everyone knows a motorcycle is approaching and they look for it. That keeps me safer. It is not a crime to ride a motorcycle.

A bad day fishing is not necessarily better than a good day at work.

A good day fishing is better than a good day at work.

Just because I do it, doesn't mean you should - At the same time just because you do it doesn't mean I should. What works for you may not work for me and vice versa. It doesn't mean we shouldn't try new things. We should.

MOLLY HATCHET - nuf said.

Steak is meant to be served extra rare.

Taters should be fried, mashed or baked.

There's room for all God's creatures - right next to the taters. Preferably fried.

Try it - You might like it. If you don't, at least you know for sure.

I am a radical.

One last thought.

I do not want to die with a gun in my hand. I cannot stand up to a tank, an A-10 Warthog or even one US soldier. I do not want to.

I do not want to live as a slave either.

Jesus said those who live by the sword shall die by the sword. I am not living by the gun. God said we may take arms to defend ourselves in others. See Nehemiah.

If I must die with a gun in my hand, I pray God will let my corpse be found in an enormous pile of spent brass and the approach to me is covered with the corpses of those who tried to kill me first.